A SHORT GUIDE TO ROMAN LONDON

ANDREW TIBBS

AMBERLEY

For Ian and Marjorie

Also by the same author:

A Short Guide to Hadrian's Wall
The Final Frontier: Scotland's Early Roman Landscape

First published 2024

Amberley Publishing
The Hill, Stroud
Gloucestershire, GL5 4EP

www.amberley-books.com

British Library Cataloguing in Publication Data.
A catalogue record for this book is available from the British Library.

ISBN: 978 1 3981 1795 2 (print)
ISBN: 978 1 3981 1796 9 (ebook)

Typesetting by SJmagic DESIGN SERVICES, India.
Printed in the UK.

Contents

Acknowledgements

In the Roman period, London grew from a small military station into a vast provincial capital, and continued to expand long after the legions had departed Britannia's shores. Since then, London has grown and grown, with vast swathes of development burying the Roman remains deep beneath the modern streets. Over the centuries, pockets of history have been uncovered, revealing glimpses of life in Londinium, sometimes preserved for future generations to see, but sometimes lost to the mists of time. Antiquarians, academics, archaeologists, developers and volunteers have all added to our knowledge of the city and its Roman origins, and without their efforts *A Short Guide to Roman London* would be a much smaller and less complete book.

As ever, it has been a challenge to keep up with the latest developments in our knowledge of Roman London because of the constant construction projects and building work which often reveal more of its ancient past. Not only this, but there is an army of academics, independent researchers and volunteers who continue to study and explore the existing Roman remains and finds, and who are constantly making new connections and discoveries. There are too many of them to mention, but I am indebted to all of them, and hope that this short guide reflects their work and achievements. I would briefly like to acknowledge the conversations and support I've had from Professor Richard Hingley, Dr Alan Montgomery, the team at Amberley, and Dr Paul Bennett. Any errors in the interpretation of the archaeology and the site details are mine alone.

In this volume, the terms London and Londinium are used interchangeably but generally refer to the area around the City (the Square Mile), which was the focus of the Roman fortifications and settlement, although there were additional Roman settlements at Southwark and Shadwell. When referring to sites beyond these areas, it will be made clear in the text.

The main chronological period covered here is the Common Era (CE), previously referred to as AD. Dates prior to this are known as Before Common Era (BCE), previously referred to as BC. The period sometimes known as Anglo-Saxon (approximately CE 410 to 1066) is referred to here as early medieval, which itself is also known as Early Middle Ages.

All the images in the book are copyright of the author, unless otherwise stated. The author has compiled the maps which contain site data extracted from various sources detailed within the text, including Historic England Research Records, the Greater London Historic Environment Record, and Ordnance Survey OpenData © Crown Copyright (2023) – OS VectorMap District, os.uk/opendata/licence.

Introduction

Sometime around the middle of the first century CE, the first Romans arrived in the area which would become London, probably around Westminster where various prehistoric routes converged at a crossing point over the River Thames. They may have been merchants keen to take advantage of the easy access afforded by the waterway, or possibly traders eager to sell their wares to passing travellers. We may not know who the earliest Roman occupants of Londinium were, but we know that the settlement grew rapidly, while another sprung up across the river at Shadwell. Before long,

The London Wall at Tower Hill.

the small settlement had grown into a bustling town, which expanded further once the Roman army arrived and established a fort on the north side of the Thames, in the area that would become Central London. Following the army were more civilians, initially comprising the slaves and families of the soldiers, but soon others arrived eager to alleviate the soldiers of their pay. Within a few decades, the settlement that started out as a shanty town had become a hub of the empire and a Roman powerhouse. Londinium became the capital of Britannia.

But our knowledge of Londinium is fragmented and piecemeal, like having a jigsaw where you find the pieces occasionally, have no picture on the box, and not all the pieces fit together. Centuries of development on top of the ruins of the Roman settlement has led to its burial, many metres below the modern streets, with small sections being rediscovered when the developers move in to build the latest skyscrapers. That's usually when we locate bathhouses, mosaics, wharfs and temples, with some of the most interesting finds having come from large-scale infrastructure projects such as Crossrail. Slowly, we're building a much more accurate picture of what life was like in Londinium almost 2,000 years ago.

A Short Guide to Roman London is not intended as an in-depth archaeological or historical book, as there are other volumes (including a significant number of archaeological reports) which fulfil this purpose. Instead, it is a short guide for those who want to explore both the surviving and visible remains of London's Roman past, and for those who want to stand in the footsteps of the citizens of Londinium and know what remains are beneath their feet, albeit several metres below and out of sight. This book is aimed at visitors and casual explorers who want to know more about London's Roman past, and some of the sites a little further afield that can be visited in a day. Hopefully, it contains something for everybody.

Glossary of Terms

Apse	Semicircular recess which frequently would have had a vaulted ceiling, and often found in bathhouses, churches and temples.
Aqueduct	A small channel used to bring water to forts, towns and buildings such as bathhouses.
Artefacts	Objects or remains, such as pottery or coins, which help archaeologists tell the story of a site.
Auxilia	Auxiliary soldiers garrisoning forts. These were paid mercenaries recruited from around the empire and who did not have Roman citizenship.
Barracks	Accommodation blocks for soldiers within the forts.

Bastion	A building-like structure, almost like a tower, which would have been attached to the London Wall, projecting outwards and used to defend it.
BCE	Before the Common Era (previously referred to as BC).
Britannia	The Roman province covering England, Wales and parts of Scotland. Originally, Londinium was the capital of the province.
CE	Common Era (previously referred to as AD).
Corinthian	An architectural style with classical origins, with main design features including acanthus leaves. This style is often found on carvings at the top of columns in buildings.
Dendrochronology	Analysis of tree rings which indicate when a piece of wood was felled, and therefore when a building was constructed.
Ditch	The wide channel which ran on the outside of the London Wall, adding an extra hazard for attackers.
Earthworks	Lumps and bumps in the ground caused by physical remains beneath the surface.
Enclosure	An area secured by a wall or similar physical boundary.
Epigraphy	The study of inscriptions.
Excavation	The archaeological process of uncovering a buried historical site.
Finds	See artefacts.
Fort	A local base for infantry and/or cavalry (horse riding soldiers), and which vary in size.
Fortress	A base for legionary soldiers (i.e. York, Chester, Lincoln).
Horrea/Horreum	A granary building, found in forts and used to store grain.
Hypocaust	An underfloor heating system with distinct remains (a raised floor supported by small pillars). Usually found in bathhouses, wealthy homes, and the *praetorium* in forts.

Indigenous	The people who originally occupied Britain before the Romans arrived.
Infantry	Foot soldiers.
Legionaries	Soldiers officially based in legionary fortresses.
London Wall	The substantial barrier which encircled the Roman settlement of Londinium. After the Romans left, the wall was adapted and strengthened and continued to be used until the eighteenth century.
Mansio	A type of government-owned hotel found outside some forts and settlements, and which was used by officials on imperial business.
Masonry	Pieces of building remains – often rubble but can also be sections of wall.
Mosaic	A piece of flooring which comprises small pieces of stone (*tesserae*) to form a decorative pattern. Mosaics as usually found in public buildings, bathhouses and high-status houses.
Praetorium	A courtyard-style building occupied by the commanding officer and their family within a fort.
Principia	The headquarters building in the centre of a fort which had an administrative, religious and financial role.
Ramparts	The walls surrounding a fortification which can either be built of turf or stone.
Tessellate	Similar to a mosaic, this is a style of decoration with a pattern of repeated shapes.
Tesserae	Individual fragments, which are usually square and made of stone, and which are laid together on a floor to create patterns.
Villa	Often thought of as a large country estate for the wealthy, with a main house and often ancillary buildings such as accommodation for workers and bathhouses. But a villa can also be a simpler agricultural estate with a farmhouse.

Part 1: A Timeline of Roman London

Romans on the Queenhithe Mosaic.

55 BCE	The first invasion of Britain by the Romans takes place under the command of Julius Caesar, but the invasion has limited success.
54	Caesar leads a second, more successful invasion and establishes diplomatic ties with tribes in southern Britain. However, once 'conquered', he withdraws from Britain back to Gaul (France).

CE 40   Emperor Caligula plans an invasion of Britain which never takes place.

43   Emperor Claudius invades Britain. It is more successful than previous attempts, and the emperor begins a programme of annexation of southern England, which takes the next seventeen years to complete.

47   The Romans attempt to assert control over the Iceni tribe (based around modern East Anglia). The tribe revolt against Roman rule, but the uprising is brief and fails.

c. 48   Date of the earliest known Roman activity in the London area, leading to the foundation of Londinium.

c. 52   Earliest Roman bridge across the River Thames.

57   Date on the earliest known correspondence/writing tablet sent from Roman Britain.

60/61   Boudica of the Iceni tribe begins a rebellion against the Romans. She, and her followers, massacre Roman citizens, burning the settlements at Londinium (London), Verulamium (St Albans) and Camulodunum (Colchester) to the ground.

c. 62/70   The first mentions of 'Londinio' (London), found on a writing tablet.

63   An early Roman fort is constructed on the north side of the River Thames.

69   Vespasian, former commander of the invasion of Britain under Claudius, becomes emperor, heralding the Flavian period of rule. In this period Londinium rapidly expands and many public buildings are constructed.

c. 70   The basilica forum is founded along with the amphitheatre.

c. 90–120   The basilica forum and the amphitheatre are expanded.

117   Publius Aelius Hadrianus (Hadrian) becomes emperor.

c. 120–150 The fort at Cripplegate is constructed.

122   Hadrian arrives in Britain (probably at Londinium) on a tour of inspection and orders the construction of Hadrian's Wall, a barrier running across northern England. It is intended to separate the barbarians from the Romans.

125–135	Some evidence for a major fire across Londinium, reducing many buildings to ash.
138	Fulvius Aelius Hadrianus Antoninus Augustus Pius (Antoninus Pius) becomes emperor, succeeding Hadrian who dies at his villa in Balae on the Bay of Naples, Italy.
c. 190–225	The London Wall is initially constructed.
211	Britannia is divided into two Roman provinces, with Londinium becoming capital of the south.
c. 240	The Temple of Mithras is first established.
c. 250	The Roman barge at Blackfriars sinks.
255	City walls of Londinium are completed.
367	Emperor Theodosius arrives in Britain to quell a barbarian uprising in the north.
c. 380	The Temple of Mithras is abandoned.
c. 383	Magnus Maximus declares himself emperor and rules Britain, Spain and Gaul, withdrawing soldiers from northern England. His rule ends when he is executed in 388.
410	Roman rule in Britain officially ends and the army is withdrawn, but in reality this is a gradual process, taking place over several years.
c. 500	Lindenwic, the early medieval successor to Londinium, emerges near the Strand.
597	An early medieval bishopric is established in London.
886	Alfred the Great arrives at Queenhithe and establishes a new settlement on the site of Londinium.
1070s	William the Conqueror begins work on a new fortress which will become the Tower of London.
c. 1200s	The ditch in front of the Roman-period London Wall is recut in places.
1665	Last outbreak of plague in London.

1666   The Great Fire of London.

1760–67   Most of the original gates through the London Wall are demolished.

1940–41   Heavy bomb damage during the Blitz, and subsequent site clearance and rebuilding works lead to the discovery of Roman sites and parts of the London Wall which were previously unknown.

1954   The Temple of Mithras is rediscovered.

1957   A large, 60-metre-long section of London Wall is uncovered during the construction of the road of the same name, and the adjacent underground car park. Only the section in the London Wall Car Park is saved.

1962   The Temple of Mithras is reconstructed on Queen Victoria Street. It is removed in 2011 and eventually rebuilt at its original location underneath the Bloomberg site in 2017.

1984   The London Wall Walk is established by the Museum of London.

1988   The Roman amphitheatre underneath the Guildhall is discovered.

2009–22   The Crossrail development brings many Roman archaeological discoveries to light.

Part 2: A Short Overview of Londinium

A doorway through the London Wall at Cooper's Row.

For centuries, London has dominated this part of the world. It has been an imperial centre, a powerhouse of trade and commerce, and a destination not to be missed; for millions, it is the place they call home. Over time the buildings and occupants may have changed, but the city is just as culturally and socially diverse today as it was almost 2,000 years ago when the first Roman citizens opted to settle in the area. In those days, the River Thames would have been much wider and shallower than it is today and geoarchaeological and archaeological evidence has indicated that there were several islands in the middle of the watercourse. Eventually, these would be bridged, occupied and gradually subsumed into the riverbanks, forming a riverscape more familiar to modern citizens, but more importantly, providing a perfect space for Londinium to grow into.

Pre-Roman Londinium

There is little evidence for prehistoric and even pre-Roman activity in the immediate area of the City of London. Perhaps then, given that so much of the city's past is buried so deeply and rarely brought to light, it is unsurprising that its early secrets remain hidden. However, occasional evidence from the time before the Romans comes to light, more often than not, from the Thames itself. One such example, which can be seen in the British Museum is the Battersea shield, a bronze shield face discovered in the river, dating to between 350 and 50 BCE. It has intricate designs and fine metalwork, suggesting it was commissioned by someone with wealth and power, although how it came to be lost or deliberately deposited in the Thames is a mystery.

Going back further than this, archaeologists working on the Thames Discovery Programme in 2010 identified a series of river timbers on the foreshore at Vauxhall in Central London that were dated to the Mesolithic period, some 6,500 years ago, although it is not clear what sort of structure they were originally a part of. Meanwhile, a short distance away are the remains of a Bronze Age timber structure, probably a jetty, which was 1,500 years old.

Another glimpse of pre-Roman activity comes from Harper Road in Southwark, where, in 1979, the body of a female aged twenty-one to thirty-eight years old was uncovered. She may have been someone with wealth and status because of several grave goods which were buried with her, originating in Continental Europe, although why she was buried here and whether she lived nearby was unclear.

What was happening in the area before the arrival of the Romans remains lost in the mists of time, and no doubt future construction work will open up more windows on the past. Perhaps, one day, we will have a better idea of what was happening in and around London before the Romans arrived, and maybe we will find out exactly what drew them to this part of the Thames. With all the major construction projects going on in the area, it seems like it is only a matter of time before further evidence is uncovered which will radically alter our understanding of London before the Romans.

Many modern cities in Britain and Europe have their origins in pre-Roman or Iron Age (*c.* 750 BCE to CE 43) settlements which grew out of farmsteads and early trading posts before expanding and evolving into Romanised towns and cities. However, Londinium appears to be the exception; one of the few towns which just appeared out of nowhere. On the eve of the first invasions, Roman writers tell us in books which have survived the centuries, there was a large indigenous population in the south-east of England. This were split into different tribal groups; the Catuvellauni occupied modern Bedfordshire, Hertfordshire and parts of Middlesex and had their capital near St Albans, while the Trinovantes, the most dominant tribe in the south-east, occupied parts of Essex, Suffolk and north-east London, and had their capital at Camulodunum (modern Colchester). The Regni were based in south London, Sussex and Surrey, and further afield, the Atrebates were based in the upper Thames valley with a base at Silchester in Berkshire. The Cantii were Canterbury based, and the Iceni (which became well known for leading revolts against the Romans, particularly by their Queen, Boudica) occupied East Anglia.

There is little evidence for any large early settlements in the London area, although it is likely that there were many indigenous routes through the area; some evidence for prehistoric trackways in south London has come to light in recent years, and which were probably 'modernised' by the Romans to become part of their road network. It is likely that these indigenous routes converged somewhere in the vicinity of Westminster, where there was a ford crossing the Thames. Surrounding these roads may have been small settlements and farmsteads. Perhaps some industrious individuals set up roadside stalls for travellers, which might have attracted more traders leading to the development of a small hamlet. That might have developed into a village, giving us the origins of Londinium. Although the archaeological evidence for this is scant, with the River Thames, and the rivers which flowed into it, acting as a natural boundary between tribal lands, it is likely that there would have been some Iron Age activity in the Central London area, while further afield there is evidence of slightly larger defended settlements, such as the early indigenous fort at Loughton Camp and Ambresbury Banks, both in the Epping Forest area in north-east London.

The Romans Arrive

Although Julius Caesar attempted to invade Britain in 55 and 54 BCE, neither of these campaigns were particularly successful. It is not until almost 100 years later that there is a successful invasion when the Emperor Claudius arrives somewhere on the south-east coast of England with a 40,000-plus-strong army. He quickly secures the territories occupied by the Cantii, and establishes his own administrative centre at Camulodunum, the tribal centre of the Trinovantes.

Within a few years, the Romans had occupied the area covered by Central London, with scientific evidence suggesting that the earliest Roman settlement was established by around CE 48. The growth of this settlement was rapid, and largely due to its positioning on the River Thames, it becomes the capital of the province, a role formerly held by Camulodunum. Londinium's rise to power has begun.

The Military Presence

The archaeological evidence suggests that Londinium started as a small trading post or a settlement focussed around a marketplace. This was probably due to its positioning on the River Thames, which at that time was much wider than it is today. Along with the extensive tidal reach, it would have helped traders move up and down the waterway with ease, facilitating the growth and expansion of trade networks from beyond the local area, and aided by the pre-Roman road network which converged around Westminster. Surprisingly, the archaeological evidence indicates that it is not until just after the middle of the first century CE that there is a military presence in the area, with the first Roman fort being constructed at Londinium. A substantial proportion of towns in the Roman world begin life as settlements which begin life next to Roman forts. The occupants would include the soldiers' families and slaves, and there would also have been traders supplying goods and services to the soldiers. Forts are essentially regional military command centres, with around 500 soldiers stationed within these. It is a secure enclosure with buildings within, surrounded by a series of walls built out of turf (known as ramparts) and a ditch in front of each of them. Within each fort were granary buildings, known as *horreum*, along with accommodation for the commanding officer (*praetorium*), barracks for the regular soldiers and a headquarters (*principia*) building which held the treasury, religious shrine and administration rooms.

Only a small section of Londinium's first fort has been uncovered, beneath Plantation Place (EC3R 7AA). Dating to around CE 63, it was uncovered during construction work, revealing the north-eastern corner of the fort defences, a double rampart with a walkway on top, along with ditches which would have been 3 metres deep. Within the ramparts part a granary building was discovered, along with a toilet block or latrine. Although only part of the site was uncovered, archaeologists have argued that this is enough to confirm the site was a fort. Some archaeologists have questioned this because the excavators found no evidence of the barrack buildings. Instead, some suggest that the site may have been a temporary camp or part of an annexe, a type of enclosure attached to military sites. Evidence uncovered during the excavations indicates the fort was occupied for around a decade, and that it had been completely abandoned by CE 85 when new, non-military buildings were constructed on the site.

A second Roman fort was later constructed at Londinium, sometime between CE 120 and 150. It was only rediscovered in the late 1940s and excavated over several decades. Subsequent development works have led to the discovery of further parts of the fort, such as the gates. The Cripplegate fort lies a little to the north-east of the amphitheatre and covers an area of around 4.5 hectares. For a Roman site in the centre of London, much is known about the fort, with the original excavations uncovering the ramparts, ditch, corner towers and some of the interior barrack buildings. The walls of the fort were eventually incorporated into the city wall when it was constructed, and it is possible to see the additional section of masonry added onto the original stonework at Noble Street Gardens (see the separate entry). This is the only place where it is possible to see part of the remains of London's Roman fort, although sadly it is quite neglected. Archaeologists speculate the fort was constructed to house the soldiers who had the task of protecting the Roman Governor of Britannia, especially as the fort was close to the building known as the Governor's Palace. The fort appears to have been redeveloped on several occasions throughout its lifetime, but was abandoned by around CE 150.

The Boudican Revolt

There is speculation that the fort at Plantation Place was built to beef up security in the aftermath of the Boudican revolt. Taking place around CE 60/61, the revolt was an indigenous uprising which led to the destruction of several Roman towns, the massacre of many citizens and caught the army on the back foot. The revolt began with the death of Prasutagus, leader of the Iceni tribe, who left half his kingdom to the emperor and half to his family. Not satisfied with half, the Emperor Nero instructed his soldiers to take all of their lands. Prasutagus' family resisted, resulting in his wife Boudica being flogged and his daughters raped. Understandably, Boudica wanted revenge, and it was fortunate for her that the Roman army was 250 miles away, campaigning in north Wales. The Governor of Britannia, Suetonius Paulinus, assumed that the tribes were loyal to Rome, and sufficiently indoctrinated into the ways of the empire to cause any trouble. But Boudica had united those dissatisfied by Rome, and they descended on the Roman settlements en masse at Colchester, London and St Albans, destroying buildings and burning the towns to the ground. Everyone within was slaughtered. Paulinus quickly hastened back, confronting the Boudican army in a final battle somewhere to the north-west of London. What happened to Boudica is unknown. Some accounts claim she poisoned herself after the battle, not wanting to be captured by the enemy, while others state that she died due to illness. Her final resting place is lost, and we may never know what really happened to her.

The Boudican revolt had a serious impact on Roman Britain, and as a result security was improved and the many public buildings that had been destroyed or damaged were rebuilt and repaired. Archaeologists working in Colchester, St Albans and London often find a layer of burning and building debris when excavating, attributing it to the damage done in the Boudican revolt.

The London Wall

Across the Roman Empire, many cities, towns and some smaller settlements built walls around their perimeters. This had the dual purpose of defining the limits of the town's jurisdiction, which was particularly important to the Romans, but also walls gave much needed protection to those within them. Londinium was no different to other Roman towns, such as St Albans, Chester and York, all of which had protective walls surrounding them. Built to withstand attacks, these walls lasted well beyond the Roman period, and were frequently strengthened and reused until the eighteenth and even nineteenth centuries. Surrounding Londinium, the London Wall, as it is now known, has its origins in the second century CE, was improved in the third century, rebuilt in the early medieval period and survived until the 1760s when parts of it, particularly the gates, were removed to improve access into the city, with much of the stone removed for reuse in new buildings. The Wall has had a lasting impact on the landscape of London, with the Roman and the medieval towns growing up within its confines (although the settlement expanded beyond its boundaries) and keeping the same layout today. Indeed, the boundary of the City of London is more or less within the line of the Wall.

Sections of the Wall still exist and can be seen on the ground, although most of what is visible dates to the early medieval adaptations to it, with the Roman foundations often visible below this. Initially, a trench was dug which was filled with clay to form a firm base on top of which large blocks of sandstone were placed. This gave the Wall a stable foundation layer, onto which were placed layers of smaller stone – usually Kentish ragstone (a type of limestone). Every few levels, a layer of Roman tiles was added for additional stability, and these can usually be seen at the lower levels of the London Wall. The Roman wall stood to a height of almost 4.5 metres and was around 2.5 to 3 metres thick, and it has been speculated that there was a wooden walkway running along the top of the Wall for its entire length, allowing guards to patrol it. Accompanying the Wall on its outer side was a ditch, acting as an added layer of defence; anyone attacking the Wall would have to cross the ditch first, no mean feat given it was around 5 metres wide and 2 metres deep. While the London Wall surrounded most of Londinium, there was initially no protection on the side facing the River Thames, probably because it was felt that the waterway itself was enough to slow down or prevent attackers. But by the late third century this had changed and the Thames Wall was constructed. Little is known about this and how it worked, as the evidence suggests it cut off access to the wharves and quays, which would have made it impractical, but perhaps this outweighed the threat of waterborne attack to the settlement.

At regular intervals along the London Wall (and probably not the Thames Wall) are a type of defensive tower known as a bastion. Constructed against the Wall, but not physically built into it, it is generally assumed they were added after the initial phases of construction. Twenty-one bastions exist, although there may have been more. While most of them were built by the Romans, some may have been added during the early medieval refurbishment. Access through the Wall and into Londinium was strictly controlled, and gates were built to manage this. Most gates were larger, enabling vehicular access, such as carts, but some were smaller and would have been for pedestrians only. Today, only the names of the Roman gates survive in the modern streets of London, such as Aldgate, Bishopgate, Cripplegate, Newgate and Ludgate. An additional gate, Aldersgate (between Cripplegate and

Newgate), appears to have been inserted into the Wall in the middle of the fourth century, while after the Roman period gates were inserted at Moorgate and by the Tower of London (Postern Gate).

Life in Londinium

Life for those in and around Londinium was heavily influenced by the River Thames. The ford at Westminster and the convergence of various routes through the landscape in this area was shaped by the Thames. The ability of ships and therefore traders and merchants, as well as migrants, to easily reach this location by water meant that the conditions were perfect for a settlement to be established here. Timbers found by the River Thames at Westminster have been dated, using dendrochronology, to the middle of the first century suggesting that wharves or quays may have been under construction at the same time as the settlement was being established. Evidence from slightly further downriver, near Queenhithe and Upper Thames Street, has indicated that quays, warehouses and wharves were soon established in the area later in the first century. Activity at Custom House and possibly Fish Street Hill (see the entry for St Magnus the Martyr) indicates the importance of both trade and the river on the growth and development of Londinium.

The importance of the Thames in Londinium's rise to power is reflected in the construction of one particularly important public building which faced onto the waterway. Towards the end of the first century CE (or possibly at the beginning of the second century), the so-called Governor's Palace was constructed close to Cannon Street station. With painted wall plaster and other objects uncovered during excavation, the indication is that this is a high-status building, an argument strengthened because of the size of the building and the number of rooms. At the time of its discovery, archaeologists thought that the only person with the power and wealth to order the construction of such as building would have been the Governor of Britannia, the emperor's man on the ground, particularly given the proximity of the Cripplegate fort which was in use at the same time and may have housed his bodyguard. Other than the area which was excavated around Cannon Street station, little other work has taken place here to reveal more about this structure, but some archaeologists now argue that it was more of an administrative building, rather than an imperial residence. Only further excavations are likely to shed more light on this impressive structure and its role within the province and city.

On the south side of the River Thames a Roman settlement was established at Southwark, seemingly after the founding of Londinium. Centred on Borough High Street, there is archaeological evidence for a substantial public building facing onto the water, underneath the more recent ruins of Winchester Palace. Nearby, substantial and impressive mosaics found at the Liberty of London site hint at Roman Southwark being a very wealthy community. Like its neighbour on the northern side of the river, the settlement at Southwark grew quickly into a trading community, but one where there was enough wealth and power to commission large buildings with status symbols such as ornate floor and wall decorations as well as bathhouses. And like Londinium, this was largely due to the settlement's position on the Thames, and because of a pre-Roman network of routes converging nearby. Again, the ease with which shipping could sail up the Thames would have led to traders and economic migrants flocking to the area, particularly from other nearby Roman territories such as Gaul. No doubt Roman Southwark still has many secrets to give up.

Shadwell also seems to have been another settlement which developed near to Londinium, and which had wealthy occupants. Although there have been limited excavations in the Shadwell area, what has been uncovered suggests there was some money here. Like Southwark, it may have originally been established as a trading post with a market, or perhaps where goods destined for the markets of Londinium were offloaded from the River Thames. The settlement dates to the early third century, perhaps when the ports of Londinium were on the wane. An ornate bathhouse has been uncovered from that period – one of the largest such structures discovered in Britain. It must have either belonged to a very wealthy citizen or senior official or was attached to a major public building. Not enough work has been undertaken in the area to indicate why such a substantial building was located here, so it remains an intriguing mystery.

Quality of life for those living in Londinium would have been very much dependent on their social status, as well as what they were doing for a living. The archaeological evidence for domestic dwellings in London is more limited for those living at the lower end of society, partly because it's difficult to identify the purpose of a building when excavated. Occasionally, within a building, archaeologists will uncover domestic items, but they can also find evidence of industrial activity within the same structure which could either suggest a workshop or that some buildings had a dual purpose as a home. Looking at evidence of domestic living from elsewhere in the empire, such as Rome, it suggests that Londinium would have been a busy, crowded mix of people from different cultures and places, some from the local area and others from as far afield as Africa and the Middle East. Within each home, it wouldn't have been any less crowded with different generations of family, as well as slaves, lodgers and even animals, living together under one roof.

Life for those at the other end of the social scale would have been quite different, with these individuals more obvious in the archaeological record as it is much easier to identify a wealthy home than it is a poor one because of the high-status goods and decorations found at such sites. We have already seen that grand buildings were constructed in Londinium, Southwark and Shadwell, evidenced from bathhouses, painted wall plaster and ornate mosaic floors – all signs of wealth. Such decorative features were created by talented artisans who worked across the empire and would not have been cheap. Commissioning them could only be afforded by the wealthiest of citizens looking to show off how rich they were.

Roman London, like the rest of the empire, was a place of contrasts. At the one end were the wealthy citizens, who had money and could afford to show it off by having the finest objects and decorations in their homes. But at the other end were the poor who had little money and even less to show for it, making them almost indistinguishable when it comes to telling the story of the masses in Londinium using the archaeology.

Religion in Londinium

The archaeological evidence from Londinium suggests that religion played an important part in the lives of those living within the city, as it did across the empire. Within the boundaries of modern London, many examples of the importance of religion have been uncovered. Various religions and cults were active in the area. A flagon uncovered in Southwark was inscribed with the words, 'Londini Ad Fanum Isis' which translates as 'To London at the Temple of Isis'. Isis was an Egyptian goddess who continued to be worshiped in the Greek and Roman periods. On the other bank of the Thames there is a legend that the grand Cathedral of St Paul's is built upon the site of a Roman temple to the goddess Diana, although this seems to be largely based on an antiquarian myth. Further outside of the confines of the City, at Greenwich Park, a Romano-British temple still survives as a grassy mound which has been excavated on a number of occasions. Built around CE 100, it was in use for around 300 years, although it is not clear who it was dedicated to, or who would have worshipped there (see the separate entry).

The most well-known and impressive surviving remains belong to the Temple of Mithras (known as a *mithraeum*), now located underneath the Bloomberg Building in Central London. Mithraism was a religion which has its origins in the east of the empire and was popular among members of the military. It took hold in the first century and remained popular for several hundred years, before Christianity rose as the dominant religion in the empire. Mithras is often equated with Sol, the sun god, who is often depicted slaying a bull, and the temples are subterranean or partly underground, representing the cave where the bull was slaughtered. Few Mithraic temples are known to have existed in Britain which makes the London one particularly important. Other examples can be found at several locations on Hadrian's Wall in the north of England, while another was at Inveresk, near Edinburgh. Although the London Mithraeum was reconstructed from the remains of the temple rediscovered in the twentieth century, the new visitor centre, which opened in 2017, has been designed as an immersive experience to give you a feel of what it would have been like as a Roman visitor to the temple.

Death in Londinium

Death is the one certainty in life, and even the great Roman city of Londinium succumbed to it. For the citizens of Roman London, everyday life was hazardous, and death lurked around every corner. Human remains have been uncovered across the city, sometimes in cemeteries, but sometimes lone burials have come to light in the strangest of places. During the construction of No. 30 St Mary Axe (otherwise known as the Gherkin skyscraper), the body of a young Roman woman was uncovered. Little is known about her or why she was buried on her own, except that she was a woman under the age of forty.

More recently, a stone sarcophagus was uncovered at a site in Southwark in 2017. Archaeologists believe it belonged to a wealthy citizen, but when they lifted the lid on it, all they found was a pile of earth. Someone had stolen the body a long time ago. A similar discovery was made near Spitalfields Market a few years earlier in 1999. Again, a stone sarcophagus was uncovered, but this time there was something more surprising within, another coffin. This one was made of lead and was intricately designed. Within that were the remains of a woman wrapped in damask silk, which had purple woven through it. Given that purple was an expensive dye and almost exclusively used by nobility or members of the upper echelons of Roman society, the woman has become known as 'Spitalfields Princess'. Close to where she was found, archaeologists have discovered a Roman burial site, although curiously it only contained males and infants, leading archaeologists to believe there may be an undiscovered separate burial site for females nearby. Almost 500 Roman burials have been recorded in the Spitalfields area.

We know very little about the Romans buried underneath London, with tantalising insights coming from their remains or the goods buried with them. Occasionally, we get more than a glimpse into their lives from epigraphic inscriptions on tombstones and altars. These memorials can tell us who was interred, who erected the memorial and even where they were from and their social status. However, most inscriptions found in London are fragments, broken stones which have been reused in new buildings or even the London Wall. One such marker records the death of the Provincial Procurator of Britannia, Julius Classicianus. The Provincial Procurator was one of the most important officials in the province, but that does not seem to have mattered to the later generations who smashed up the tombstone and used it in the construction of the London Wall.

Londinium's End

It is said that Roman rule of Britannia ended in CE 410, although the empire actually began its withdrawal of soldiers and resources from the province decades beforehand. As such, Roman rule gradually faded rather than there being a precise date when the army withdrew from these shores. Nor did life in Londinium cease in 410. The city had certainly changed since the height of its powers in the second and third centuries. The population had declined, the wealth and power had faded away, and there were more attacks on the capital from those living elsewhere in Britain, but also from those outside of the empire. There were still people living in amongst the crumbling ruins of Londinium; bathhouses were long since abandoned and filled up with rubbish. There was no one to keep the peace. Civic buildings were falling down and even basic services such as sewers and aqueducts were collapsing, with no one with the skills to repair them left. The lack of a military presence would have led to a power vacuum, which was filled by local gangs and warlords, eager to create their own fiefdoms, and there was no one to stop them. Ordinary citizens would have feared for their lives, trying to avoid the bandits roaming the streets, or the pirates raiding from the Thames. With attacks on the empire from those living outside its borders, such as the Picts, Angles, Saxons and Goths, increasing, life in post-Roman Londinium would have been considerably different. The Roman Empire had left Britannia and Londinium to the fates.

Part 3: Visiting Roman London

The London Wall.

The main areas of Roman activity in Londinium centred around what is now the City of London, although there are many other sites and museums further afield in Central and Greater London and beyond. Most of these can easily be visited in a day, although some places visitors might want to spend more time in to get a proper feel for the area.

This book has been written to help visitors decide what can be seen, what there is to do and how to get there. Whether you are a casual day tripper, dedicating a few days to exploring London or even just passing through on the way elsewhere, it has something for everyone.

Maps

Many of the archaeological sites detailed in this volume, particularly those around Central London, are not on the standard Ordnance Survey (OS) Explorer map series, although some are on the official OSMaps app. However, visitors will find it helpful to have access to a detailed map, such as an A–Z guide, the OSMap app or another detailed map covering London when exploring the sites in and around the City and Central areas. For visiting sites beyond Central London, OS maps are recommended. Where possible, directions to access the archaeological sites have been included in the individual site descriptions, but it is recommended that visitors plan their visits especially as public transport can be limited to some sites and parking restrictive.

Transport

London has some of the best transport networks in the UK, and it is possible to see many sites in and around the City using these and on foot, although it can be exhausting. Most sites are connected by bus, although the easiest way to jump between them is via the London Underground, with the nearest Tube station to each site detailed in the listings. For those sites which are in Greater London or beyond, the nearest London Overground or mainline rail station is listed.

For details of travel within London (Underground, Overground, bus and taxi), including a handy journey planner, download the TfL Go app or visit tfl.gov.uk. For details of travel to sites beyond London, visit nationalrail.co.uk.

Accessibility

Accessibility at sites around London is generally good for those with limited mobility, particularly most of the larger museums and visitor sites. Some smaller or older buildings, such as the churches, can be more restrictive and lack lifts and other accessibility features. General accessibility of sites in parklands is generally good, although physical remains can often be off-path and accessed via uneven terrain, which can be muddy and wet. Accessible facilities such as toilets or cafes may also be limited at the various sites. Where possible, accessibility has been detailed in the text, but it is recommended that visitors check site websites or contact the venue for further information, including accessibility statements.

Some London Underground stations have limited access for those with mobility issues, and it is helpful to plan routes in advance using the TfL Go app which details accessibility at each stop. Where relevant, the nearest Underground station to a site is indicated here in the text, but this can still involve a lengthy walk to a site. Travellers with mobility issues using the rail network can arrange assistance, in advance of travel, via local train operators; see the National Rail Enquiries website for further information.

Countryside Code

Many of the sites covered here can be accessed by visitors, but there are a number which are privately owned. Where possible, this has been stated in the individual site entries. For those sites which it is not possible to visit, if there is a nearby path or viewpoint from which the site can be seen, this has also been noted in the text. Some of the sites outside of Central London are set in parkland or more rural environments, and visitors are advised to check fields for livestock before accessing them, especially at those times of year when animals may be pregnant and particularly if accompanied by dogs. In England, the Countryside Code (www.gov.uk/government/publications/the-countryside-code) applies to the landscape surrounding some sites and recommends the following for visitors:

- Consideration for those living and working in or enjoying the countryside.
- Leaving gates and property as you find them.
- Not blocking access to gateways and driveways.
- Follow local signs and keep to marked paths.
- Taking litter home.
- Not lighting fires.
- Keep dogs under control.
- Bag and bin dog poo.
- Check local conditions and plan your route.

Dogs

There are few opportunities for dogs to access the indoor sites in and around Roman London, so it is worth checking individual site websites for information on access for those with four-legged friends. By law in the UK, assistance dogs are allowed access to all sites and museums.

Finding Something Roman

If you've found an object which could be Roman, then there are several things you should do. Note the National Grid Reference (using at least six digits) and location where the object was found, handle it with care and don't clean it. Take photos of the object and its location, and try to avoid touching the ground where it was found in case archaeologists want to excavate. Then contact the local Finds Liaison Officer (www.finds.org.uk/contacts) who will advise you on what to do next, or speak to the experts at your local museum.

It is important to understand that it is illegal to dig or metal-detect on a site which is legally protected as a Scheduled Monument – this includes Roman forts and most other ancient and historic sites. Mudlarking, or searching the foreshore of the River Thames (between Teddington and the Thames Barrier), is prohibited without a permit, of which only a small number are issued each year by the Port of London Authority through the Thames Estuary Mudlarking Society (www.mudlarkers.co.uk). For more information see www.pla.co.uk/Environment/Thames-foreshore-permits.

The rules surrounding mudlarking on the River Thames state that failing to declare found objects to the Portable Antiquities Scheme can be a criminal offence, so it is always best to check with the local Finds Liaison Officer who will be happy to help. A range of guides and publications aimed at supporting anyone undertaking field walking, metal detecting and mudlarking can be found at www.finds.org.uk.

Part 4: The Sites

London has a rich archaeological heritage stretching back over thousands of years. Wandering around the streets, it is easy to come across modern skyscrapers next to medieval guildhalls and Tudor-style taverns. Sections of the Roman and medieval London Wall can be found hidden between hotels and office blocks, or tucked away in leafy gardens. Occasionally, the Wall can be found deep below street level, locked away in the basements and cellars of the most unassuming buildings. Sometimes it is even possible to visit these most secret and hidden remains of the Roman settlement. But the influence of Londinium spread far out from the confines of the City and into the suburbs of London, where there are many ancient sites and wonders to be seen, from statues and temples, to villas and museums.

   This chapter focuses on the sites and museums which can be found in and around London. The sites have been grouped together into broad, geographical sections – the City of London, Central London and Greater London. A further section summarises Roman sites beyond London, but which can be comfortably visited by road or rail in a day, for those visitors who want to explore beyond the city. The sites have been numbered to correspond with the relevant map, and in the best order to visit sequentially. Each entry follows the same format:

- Site Number | Site Name.
- London Wall Walk Plaque Number (if applicable).
- Site Type(s) | Facilities | Entry Charge (if not free) | Nearest Rail Station.
- Address | Postcode | National Grid Reference | What 3 Words.
- Website.
- An overview of the site with details of which features to see.
- Site directions and accessibility.

The National Grid Reference and What 3 Words location details are the most accurate locators, as the postcodes defer to the nearest house or settlement, which can be some distance from the Roman site. It is advised to check the location on a map before setting out.

Sources
A list of sources used for the information given within individual site entries can be found in the Finding Out More section at the end of the book.

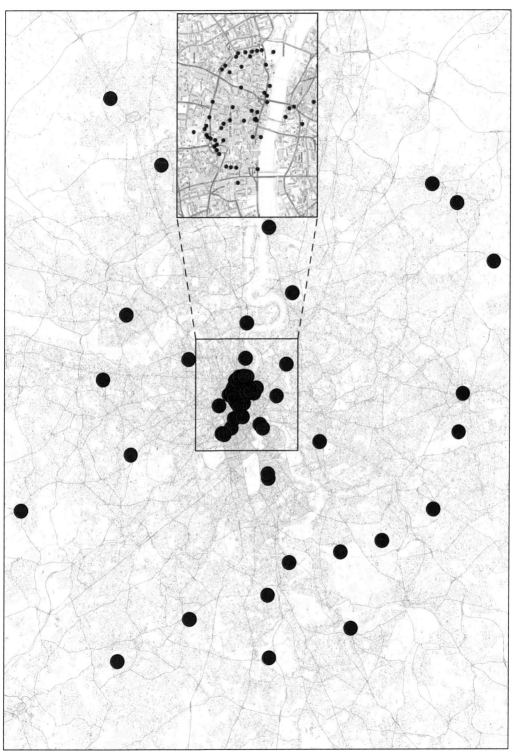

The Sites

The London Wall

Discovering London's Roman history by following the line of the ancient wall is a great way to experience the modern and historical city. In the mid-1980s, the Museum of London set out to do this by creating the London Wall Walk which followed the known line of the Wall around the edge of the City of London. Divided into sections, a tiled interpretation plaque was put in position at each one, explaining a little about that area. Originally there were twenty panels across the line of the Wall but, sadly, many of these have been lost, destroyed or stolen and only eleven survive.

It is still possible to follow the original route of the London Wall Walk, and see the surviving plaques (not all of them are in the original positions), although some sections have changed largely due to development. Copies of all the original plaques can be seen in a leaflet originally produced by the Museum of London, and which the City of London Archaeological Trust have made available on their website – www.colat.org. uk/_assets/doc/london-wall-walk-guide.pdf. The London On My Mind website (www. londonmymind.com/london-wall-walk) has an updated list of the surviving London Wall Walk plaques and where to see them. Where possible, London Wall Walk plaques have been noted in the individual site entries here.

London Wall Walk plaque at Tower Hill.

The first London Wall Walk plaque can be found at the Postern Gate, on the north side of the Tower of London, and close to the statue of the Emperor Trajan at Trinity Square (see separate entry). Not actually Roman, the Postern Gate was uncovered in 1979, and probably dates to the latter part of the thirteenth century when the moat for the Tower was dug. Smaller than the regular gates, the Postern Gate was intended for use by pedestrians. However, the construction of the moat appears to have had a significant impact on the gate, leading to its subsidence, and it partly collapsed in 1440. It was subsequently rebuilt a little further to the north, but it eventually fell out of use and was dismantled in the eighteenth century. The London Wall Walk plaque can be found on the eastern wall of the underpass, by the remains of the Postern Gate.

For more on the history and archaeology of the London Wall, see Part 2.

Crossrail
archaeology.crossrail.co.uk/exhibits

Major construction and development projects within the city are often the main way that discoveries about the past are made. As buildings become taller and bigger, deeper foundations are needed, leading to the discovery of archaeological deposits, which are often many meters below street level. In some areas of London, the Roman street level can be 5 or more meters below the modern pavement. Crossrail is one such recent project which has been particularly insightful into the past. The project, which resulted in the creation of the Underground's Elizabeth Line, took over fifteen years to construct and runs for over 100 kilometres across Central and Greater London and beyond.

Crossrail has provided a significant insight into London's past, and there have been numerous important discoveries uncovered during construction of the line. Archaeological excavations took place for the best part of a decade and involved hundreds of archaeologists. Prior to the construction of the new line, previous excavations in the 1980s at Liverpool Street station led to the discovery of human remains from the burial ground of the old Royal Bethlem Hospital (otherwise known as Bedlam), which included Roman bodies. It was therefore unsurprising to archaeologists that more bodies were discovered during the Crossrail work in the area. The site is also close to the River Walbrook, one of the waterways flowing beneath the modern city and into the Thames, with excavations uncovering wooden Roman gates which were reused as a walkway or platform next to the watercourse. This discovery was in the same area where over twenty Roman skulls were also found, with some archaeologists suggesting that they were slaughtered during the Boudican revolt and their remains dumped by the Walbrook.

Some of the discoveries from Crossrail will go on display at the new Museum of London, but there is also an online exhibition of some of the more interesting finds which can be seen at the link above. It is likely that there will be many more archaeological discoveries about London's past from other major construction projects.

City of London: East

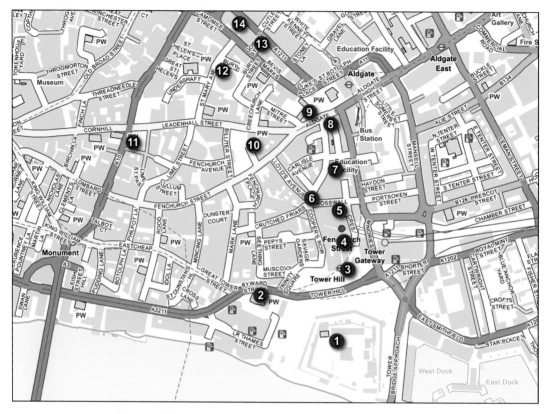

Roman sites in the east of the City of London.

For almost 2,000 years London has survived in one shape or form, so it should not be surprising that a city which became an economic and social powerhouse in the Roman period has continued to be so, with the modern City sitting on top of the remains of Londinium. The remains in the east of the City of London mainly follow the line of the Roman and medieval London Wall, with impressive sections of Roman and medieval Wall sitting in the shadows of skyscrapers.

1 | Tower of London | Tower Hill West
London Wall Walk 1
Road | London Wall | Museum | Café | Toilets | Charge | Tower Hill
EC3N 4EE | TQ 334 806 | shin.smiled.plug

The area around the Tower of London is heaving with history and archaeology. Not just in the buildings and walls that surround Tower Hill, but beneath the ground. The earliest activity in the area dates to the prehistoric period, with Bronze Age and

Mesolithic finds including flint and pottery being uncovered within the grounds of the Tower along with an Iron Age burial which was discovered during works in the 1970s. Tower Hill West, the area outside the main entrance to the Tower, where entry tickets are purchased, is also where a section of Roman road runs. The line of the road crosses close to the middle of Tower Hill West, from the direction of Highway in the east and heading westwards, with Great Tower Street running on the same alignment. Limited excavation of the area has indicated that there was Roman activity to the north and south of the road, with painted plaster found during excavations indicating there may have been high-status buildings close by, but exactly where remains unknown.

The line of the London Wall runs across the Tower of London site on a north–south trajectory and survives as ruins; these are below ground, along with traces of the Thames Wall which was on the river side of the site. To the east, traces of the ditch have been recorded, but again these are not visible. Within the Tower precinct, the layout of Inmost Ward is defined by the original line of the London Wall which surrounded Londinium on the east side. Works in the area have uncovered evidence to suggest that there were both timber and stone buildings which were occupied throughout the Roman period. The Inmost Ward, the original medieval part of the Tower (which was built by William I), consists of the Wardrobe Tower, main Guard Wall and Coldharbour Gate, the former (which is to the east of the White Tower) incorporating parts of the London Wall and utilising the base of a Roman bastion.

Where the London Wall meets the Tower of London.

In the 1950s, a new Jewel House was constructed within the grounds of the Tower. This led to the uncovering of a previously unknown section of the Roman London Wall, although it was only a few metres long, ending at the Wardrobe Tower, where the terminus was partially damaged. This has led archaeologists to conclude that the Wall had subsided some time in the past. Beyond this the remains had been destroyed by later construction in the medieval period.

Directions & Accessibility: There are no Roman remains to be seen at Tower Hill West or within the Tower of London, although some objects found within the grounds are occasionally on display. The Postern Gate (London Wall Walk 1) is to the north side of the Tower and is free to access without entering the ticketed Tower of London site. See the Trinity Square entry.

2 | All Hallows by the Tower Church
Remains | Building | Londinium Model | Museum | Tower Hill
Byward Street | EC3R 5BJ | TQ 333 806 | call.flying.remit
www.ahbtt.org.uk

Sometimes known as All Hallows Barking because the original eleventh-century church was attached to Barking Abbey, All Hallows by the Tower was originally established sometime around CE 675. Part of the original Saxon church can be seen in the crypt, which is now a museum. It was only rediscovered when the church was bombed in 1940. Within All Hallows there are various Roman remains to be seen, including two sections of Roman tessellated floor which came from a house which was established on the site by the end of the late second century. The *tesserae* tiles were laid directly onto the ground, rather than being part of a *hypocaust* heating system, and over time the individual tiles moved around and became worn and were subsequently patched up with bits of old masonry, which can still be seen in the remains today. The first piece of flooring can be seen in the foundations of the tower and was discovered when work was undertaken in the 1920s to stabilise the medieval structure. During these works, other Roman objects were recovered and are on display in the crypt museum, along with grave markers and inscriptions. Also within the crypt museum is a second piece of Roman flooring, although this was discovered elsewhere on the site, and is similar to the first section. There is also an excellent model of Londinium on display, showing the main buildings and features of the city, fort, Wall and river crossings.

As well as the Roman remains, there are many other pieces to see in the crypt, including carved stone remains and a barrel, originally part of the crow's nest from Shackleton's third ship which took him to the Antarctic. Even the crypt itself, and which was the original Saxon church at All Hallows, is worth seeing. There are regular events held at the church, and both guided and audio tours take place. The frequent organ recitals are not to be missed.

Directions & Accessibility: Located to the north-west of the Tower of London, the church itself is fully accessible, although the crypt is below street level and access is by a small, narrow staircase which may be challenging for some.

3 | Trinity Square | The Emperor Trajan Statue
London Wall Walk 2
Remains | London Wall | No Facilities | Tower Hill
Trinity Square | EC3N 4DH | TQ 335 807 | broker.gasp.milk

Sitting a little away from the Tower Hill entrance to the Underground is one of the best preserved sections of London Wall, watched over by a statue of the Roman Emperor Trajan. This section of Wall was uncovered in 1938, and runs for 12 metres and stands to a height of just under 3.5 metres. The area was discovered in the aftermath of Second World War bomb damage, while Tower Hill Gardens, on the other side of the Wall, were created around the same time. In the mid-nineteenth and early twentieth centuries, stones recovered from the foundations of the Wall were revealed to have originally been part of a tomb. An inscription on one fragment stated that the occupant of the tomb was a very high-ranking imperial official, Julius Classicianus, the Provincial Procurator (a type of finance manager) of the entire province of Britannia.

On the other side of the Wall is one of the more well-known statues in London. Created in the twentieth century, the statue depicts the Emperor Trajan, who reigned from CE 98 to 117. The statue itself has a curious past. It was installed here in the

The London Wall at Trinity Square.

1980s, but had been recovered from a Southampton scrapyard in around 1920, and is a copy of an original first-century Roman statue from southern Italy. The original is in the National Archaeology Museum in Naples. When the statue was recently analysed by archaeologists from the Museum of London, they noted that the head and body appear to be from two different statues.

Nearby, there is a hidden section of the London Wall in the basement of Wakefield House (Nos 40–41 Trinity Square). Small, but well preserved, this section is not on public display. At this point, it is also worth mentioning the nearby Postern Gate which enabled access through the London Wall. The remains of the gate are on the other side of the underpass under Tower Hill, and can be seen in front of the Tower of London (see the directions below). Although the gate dates to the medieval period, sometime around the 1270s, it probably replaced an early structure which could have been Roman. A small gate, it was for use by pedestrians, rather than carts. It partially collapsed in the 1440s and was rebuilt but only lasted until the eighteenth century.

Directions & Accessibility: On exiting Tower Hill Underground station at Trinity Square, turn right and go down the first set of steps, towards the Tower of London; the statue and London Wall are on the left. From Tower Gateway DLR station, exit and cross Minories and carry straight on, parallel with the office block on the right. When Tower Hill station is in front, turn left down the steps and the London Wall and Trajan statue are on the left. The Postern Gate, which marks the beginning of the London Wall Walk, can be found by continuing down the steps, and through the underpass. The London Wall Walk plaque can be found on the left on emerging from the underpass.

4 | Trinity Place
Remains | London Wall | No Facilities | Tower Hill | London Wall Walk 3
EC3N 2LY | TQ 336 808 | stray.copies.healers

See the entry for Cooper's Row.

5 | America Square
Remains | London Wall | No Facilities | Tower Hill
EC3N 2LS | TQ 335 809 | saying.flat.dirt

This section of the London Wall is known to have run from the appropriately named Crosswall, behind America Square, and ends somewhere underneath Fenchurch Street station, where there are also the remains of a third-century bastion. Large parts of this section of the Wall are believed to survive beneath the ground, with only one part visible above, although this is within the basement of One America Square. This section, which survives to a height of around 2 metres, was uncovered during development work in the late 1980s, and can be seen through windows within the arches of One America Square on the side it borders with Crosswall. The building is private and access restricted, but occasional visitors are allowed in to view the Wall

The London Wall beneath America Square.

by asking at reception. A little distance from the building, a 7-metre stretch of Roman road was also discovered during construction of One America Square, although this was subsequently covered up.

Directions & Accessibility: There are no visible remains to be seen, except for those within the conference centre at One America Square. Permission from One America Square is needed to access these remains.

6 | Cooper's Row
London Wall Walk 3
Remains | London Wall | No Facilities | Tower Hill
EC3N 2LY | TQ 335 809 | doctor.dots.activism

Originally hidden by buildings once owned by the notorious East India Company, a sizeable section of London Wall survives at Cooper's Row. Initially discovered in 1864 when warehouses on the site were demolished, it was soon covered up again by a new building, which was demolished in 1961, making the Wall accessible. Standing to an impressive 10.6 metres high, the lower section is Roman, with the upper parts dating to the medieval period. The distinctiveness of the Roman layers on the bottom is

Cooper's Row section of the London Wall.

obvious and quite different from the later stone work. There are several features which can be seen, including socket holes in the upper levels which would have supported a wooden walkway, windows which would have enabled archers to fire on anyone attacking, traces of staircases, and it is even possible to pass through the Wall.

Directions & Accessibility: The Wall at Cooper's Row can be a little difficult to find, but it is worth making the effort for. It can either be accessed through the open entrance of the Leonardo Royal Hotel (the Wall is visible from Cooper's Row). Alternatively, it is possible to get to the Wall through a small lane outside the entrance to Tower Hill station, behind the Citizen M Hotel. The area is fully accessible. Walking through the doorway in the Wall gives a shortcut on the way to the next entry, Crutched Friars.

7 | Crutched Friars | Emperor House
London Wall Walk 4
Remains | London Wall | Café | Toilets | Fenchurch Street
Emperor House, 12 Jewry Street | EC3N 2PX | TQ 335 810 | pushed.finest.motion
www.citywallvinestreet.org

Hidden beneath the recently rebuilt Emperor House lies an impressively well-preserved section of the London Wall. The surviving remains, which are open to the public, include a

The London Wall beneath Emperor House.

section of the Wall, around 11 metres long and 3 metres high, along with a fourth-century bastion and are well worth visiting. The Wall was excavated between 1979 and 1980, revealing the red sandstone plinth which marks street level in Roman times. Above this, layers of stone bonded with courses of red tiles are visible. The bastion, added around the latter part of the fourth century is clearly visible, with fragments of reused masonry and stone making up the walls. Tombstones were frequently used in the construction of the bastions, and in this section, fragments of an early third-century example have been identified.

Directions & Accessibility: This section of Wall is contained within the basement of the newly developed Emperor House, otherwise known as The City Wall at Vine Street. Access is from No. 35 Vine Street, although tickets (free) must be booked in advance through the website. The site is fully accessible.

8 | The Three Tuns (Aldgate)
Remains | London Wall | No Facilities | Aldgate
No. 36 Jewry Street | EC3N 2ET | TQ 335 811 | drew.legend.plays
www.bestcitypubs.co.uk/three-tuns-aldgate

It is no surprise that being located next to Centurion House, The Three Tuns has some hidden Roman history beneath its floors. The London Wall runs right beneath the

The Three Tuns pub next to the aptly named Centurion House.

eastern side of Jewry Street, with visible and buried remains beneath these buildings. The Three Tuns is no exception and a section of the London Wall, along with its Roman foundations, can be seen in the pub's beer cellar, although this is not generally accessible. There are further details of the Roman activity in the area listed under the Aldgate entry.

Directions & Accessibility: This section of London Wall is hidden in the cellars of The Three Tuns and generally not accessible to the public. Due to the historic nature of the building, access can be limited.

9 | Aldgate
London Wall | City Gate | No Facilities | Aldgate | London Wall Walk 5
EC3A 5DE | TQ 335 811 | ended.sticky.castle

There are three surviving sections of Roman Wall around Aldgate, although there is little to be seen on the ground. The first section runs from No. 17 Bevis Marks towards St James' Passage, a modern subway which cuts through the Wall.

In advance of constructing the subway, excavations showed it survived for a length of 1.7 metres at Duke's Place, 3 metres below the modern ground level. Also in this section of the wall was bastion 7, sticking out from the face of the Wall by almost 6 metres.

The second section of Roman wall runs beneath the western side of Aldgate Square, crossing over Aldgate, and running beneath Jewry Street. Various archaeological excavations and development works have confirmed it exists, although nothing is visible on the ground. This section also includes the Roman gateway at Aldgate, which had two entrances flanked by towers, and is recorded as still being used in the early medieval period. Geoffrey Chaucer, author of *The Canterbury Tales*, rented one of the rooms in the gatehouse in the fourteenth century. Also in this section of Wall were several bastions, one of which was noted by antiquarian William Maitland, in the nineteenth century, as being in perfect condition and standing to a height of over 6 metres.

The third section of Wall runs parallel with Jewry Street, ending around its intersection with India Street. A small stretch of Wall from this section is on display in nearby buildings, although development works have confirmed that further Wall foundations and a bastion survive beneath nearby streets.

Directions & Accessibility: There are no visible remains at street level. Sections survive and are visible in David Game College and The Three Tuns (see the separate entry), although these are in areas not accessible to the public.

10 | Basilica Forum
No Facilities | Fenchurch Street
EC3M 5HN | TQ 333 810 | piles.salads.flap

See Leadenhall Market.

11 | Leadenhall Market
Remains | Basilica Forum | Wall | No Facilities | Monument
Gracechurch Street | EC3V 0DN | TQ 330 810 | edgy.jungle.wake

The basilica forum in ancient Londinium would have been one of the most important buildings in the whole of the province. It had multiple functions; it was the civic, legal and administrative centre of the city, and would also have housed the treasury, numerous shrines, and had a role as a marketplace. Covering a space of 2 hectares, it was the biggest building of its type in northern Europe.

It was first discovered during the initial construction of Leadenhall Market in 1848. More recent development works in the area, along with targeted excavation, have led archaeologists to surmise what the building looked like, and its layout. They have concluded that the first tranche of Roman activity on the site was before the construction of the basilica forum took place during the first century and may have been started by the Roman army. The site was further developed around CE 50 to 60, but was destroyed

Leadenhall Market, built upon part of the site of the Roman basilica forum.

by fire during the Boudican revolt. The first forum was not constructed at the site until the latter part of the first century, but this was eventually replaced by a larger basilica and forum in the early part of the second century. The buildings seem to have survived until the fourth century when it was demolished, although a small section of the base of an arch survives and is on display in the most unlikely of locations – in the basement of Nicholson and Griffin Hairdressers in Leadenhall Market.

Directions & Accessibility: The remains are within a hairdressers and therefore access is limited, but at quiet times the friendly staff are happy to show visitors the arch. Due to the nature of the location, accessibility is restrictive.

12 | St Mary Axe (The Gherkin)
Remains | Burial | Memorial | No Facilities | Aldgate
18 Bury Street | EC3A 5AW | TQ 332 812 | paid.flap.precautions

At the foot of London's famous 'Gherkin' skyscraper lies the grave of a young Roman girl. It is not clear who she is or why she was buried on her own in the heart of Londinium. Back in the mid-1990s, when the Gherkin was being built, the skeleton was uncovered, although it is the location which in unusual. In Roman times, this would have been outside of the limits of Londinium (Roman law stipulated that burials were not permitted within the walls of a settlement). Other than her age, between thirteen and seventeen years old, almost nothing is known about who she was or why she was buried here. Artefacts found with her gave a date of the second half of the fourth century for her burial. On completion of the Gherkin, it was decided to re-inter her remains where they were discovered. Her burial is marked on the ground with a simple slate slab featuring a laurel wreath,

Grave of an unknown Roman girl at the foot of No. 30 St Mary Axe.

the symbol of Rome, along with a dedication carved into the granite stone which surrounds the base of the Gherkin. It reads:

DIS MANIBUS
PUELLA INCOGNITA
LONDINIENSIS
HIC SEPULTA EST

To the spirits of the dead
The unknown young girl
From Roman London
Lies buried here

Directions & Accessibility: The Gherkin is an unmissable landmark in this part of London, on the west side of St Mary Axe. The grave marker and memorial can be seen on the eastern side of the building, facing onto Bury Street. The marker is about halfway along the plaza outside the Gherkin. It is fully accessible.

13 | Goring Street
London Wall | Bastion | No Facilities | Aldgate
EC3A 8BG | TQ 333 813 | robot.shack.comb

The nineteenth century saw a number of Roman discoveries on Goring Street, although sadly none are visible today. In 1884, construction work led to the uncovering of a section of the Roman London Wall, over 2 metres thick and buried some 3 metres beneath the street level. Close by, on the west side of Goring Street was a bastion which reused a large amount of Roman stonework, with fragments including an inscription and a frieze with hares carved on it.

Sadly, in 1923, a 37-metre long stretch of the Wall was uncovered only 2 metres below the road surface, and which stood 2.5 metres tall, but was subsequently destroyed. In the 1970s, a fragment of Roman tombstone was discovered nearby (and subsequently lost), with a partial inscription which read 'In memory of Tulla Numidie ... a most devoted woman'.

Directions & Accessibility: There are no remains to be seen at this location.

14 | Camomile Street
London Wall | Bastion | No Facilities | Liverpool Street
EC3A 7LL | TQ 333 813 | pure.once.necks

Around 1707, at the junction of Camomile Street and Bishopsgate, a mosaic pavement was uncovered during building works. The massive mosaic extended for 18 metres and was 3 metres wide, although it was probably wider as it ran underneath other, more modern buildings which were not due to be demolished, while beneath the mosaic were several second-century cremation burials.

In the nineteenth and early twentieth centuries, construction work in this part of London led to the discovery of a bastion set into the wall, which was 6 metres wide, projected from the wall by 4.5 metres and survived to a height of 3 metres. Another nearby section of London Wall was uncovered, 2.5 metres below street level, with the remains standing to a height of just under 4.5 metres, but sadly this is not visible.

Directions & Accessibility: There are no remains to be seen in this location.

City of London: West

To the west of the City of London is a landscape rich in architecture, both ancient and modern. Sections of the London Wall, complete with decaying bastions, sit side by side with Christopher Wren-designed churches and the brutalist architecture of the Barbican Estate. Among all of this are the Roman remains, nestled pockets of gardens, oases of greenery, offering respite from the hustle and bustle of modern London.

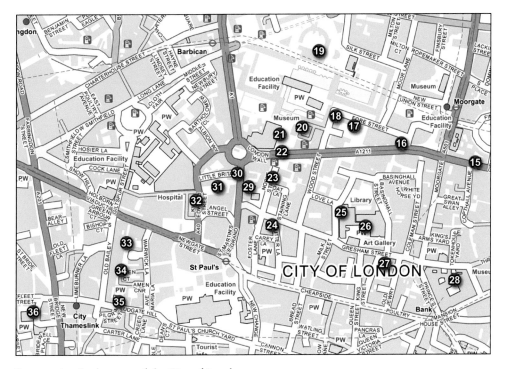

Roman sites in the west of the City of London.

15 | Moorgate
London Wall | City Gate | No Facilities | Moorgate | London Wall Walk 11
EC2M 5TR | TQ 328 815 | even.double.quiet

Unlike many of the other gates along the London Wall, Moorgate does not have its origins as an entrance into Roman Londinium. What it does have in common with the other city gates is that it was demolished in 1761 as part of attempts to improve traffic access through the ancient Wall. The area around this part of Londinium was originally marshy, but the Romans, being brilliant engineers, drained most of the landscape into the Walbrook which runs nearby. However, construction of the London Wall seems to have caused the water levels to rise, and the landscape once again became marshy. But it is not until the medieval period that a gate is put through the Wall, and by the sixteenth century, the land was once again drained, giving way to tree-lined avenues. Despite demolition of the gate, the London Wall formed part of the Bethlehem Hospital, otherwise known as Bedlam, before being completely demolished in the early nineteenth century.

There are no remains to be seen here, but the site of Moorgate is recorded on a nearby plaque. Various Roman discoveries have been made in the area, including a building with a *hypocaust*, and a tombstone found in the Walbrook with a poignant inscription: 'To Marcus Aurelius Eucarpus, my most devoted son, aged 15 years, six months. Set up by his mother.'

Directions & Accessibility: There are no remains to be seen at this location.

16 | London Wall Car Park
London Wall Walk 18
Remains | London Wall | No Facilities | Moorgate
No. 23 London Wall | EC2V 5DY | TQ 325 815 | parts.meals.cloth

A Central London car park is an unlikely location for some Roman remains, but that's exactly what can be found in a quiet corner of the suitably named London Wall Car Park. Running for around 11 metres, this is one of the better surviving sections of London Wall which can still be seen. Standing to a height of just under 4 metres, it was discovered in 1957 when the London Wall road was being built. Back then, workers uncovered a 64-metre section of Wall, 5 metres below ground level. Almost all of this was destroyed by the roadworks, and only the relatively small section in the car park was preserved.

Directions & Accessibility: Access to the car park is a little hidden and difficult to find on foot, but following the road signs will lead to it. Heading down a slope, from current-day street level to near Roman levels, the London Wall Walk plaque is outside the main entrance. Access to the car park is through the entrance to the right of this. The car park is free to access for visiting the remains on foot, although be aware that the section of London Wall is at the opposite end of the car park, and not visible

London Wall Walk plaque at the entrance to the London Wall Car Park.

until you are almost at it. There are steps to an exit from the car park a little further on from the Wall. The car park is long and thin, and although well lit, some may be uncomfortable accessing the space.

17 | St Alphage Churchyard
London Wall Walk 12
Remains | London Wall | No Facilities | Moorgate
Barbican | EC2Y 5DE | TQ 324 816 | moon.deeply.zone

Originally the site of the Church of St Alphage, the building was constructed adjoining the London Wall, which doubled up as its northern wall. The church was demolished in the 1600s, but rebuilt in the following years, lasting until the twentieth century when it fell into ruin. Its demise was hastened by First World War bomb damage and, eventually, the church was partially demolished in the 1920s, before fire finished it off two decades later. The surviving structures and the garden were refurbished and made more accessible in 2018.

The area is an oasis of calm in the city, and at the heart of the gardens are various remains of the London Wall and St Alphage's. On the north side of the gardens are the

Roman ruins at the site of the Church of St Alphage.

remains of the London Wall, while at the eastern end it is possible to see the original wall of the Cripplegate fort at the back. Lower down, at the front, are the additional layers of stone which were added when the fort wall was incorporated into the London Wall.

Directions & Accessibility: Located a little to the north of the London Wall road, and to the east of Monkwell Square, the gardens are a pleasant distraction in an area of modernist architecture. Free to access, the gardens have plenty of seating from which to admire the ancient ruins. Access is on level ground, although there are a couple of steps when getting closer to the Roman remains.

18 | Cripplegate
London Wall Walk 13
Remains | London Wall | Tower | No Facilities | Moorgate
EC2Y 8BJ | TQ 323 816 | took.putty.oils

Cripplegate, at Wood Street, was one of the old gateways through the London Wall. Lying close to Fore Street and St Alphage Garden, this would also have been the northern entrance to the Cripplegate fort, with Wood Street being on the same

The London Wall Walk plaque at the site of Cripplegate.

alignment as the *via praetoria*, one of the main streets within the fortification. Cripplegate is mentioned in the late ninth and early tenth centuries, but has never been excavated. The location of the fort gateway has been postulated from nearby excavations of the site. The Cripplegate entrance to London lasted until 1761 when it was cleared to improve access to the city. This was the fate of many of the old gates as the size of the entrances limited the amount of traffic that could pass through. The site of Cripplegate is marked by a London Wall Walk plaque on the appropriately named Roman House, which itself is built on top of the ditch which ran in front of the London Wall.

Directions & Accessibility: There are no remains to be seen at this location.

19 | Barbican Estate | St Giles Cripplegate
London Wall Walk 14 and 15
Remains | London Wall | No Facilities | Barbican
EC2Y 8DS | TQ 323 818 | tubes.rates.tried

The brutalist architecture of the Barbican Estate hides a number of historic sites, including large sections of the London Wall, remains of bastions and a medieval church, St Giles, Cripplegate. Located on the edge of Londinium and largely outside the city walls, the area's Roman history was, until the twentieth century, hidden underneath warehouses and other buildings. These were damaged by bombing in the Second World War, and the site was subsequently cleared to make way for the Barbican Estate in the 1970s.

On the south side of the estate, exposed foundations of the London Wall can be seen in the gardens, with the lake marking the site of the medieval ditch which ran parallel with the Wall, while several bastions and a possible Roman watch tower (known as a *barbicane* in Latin) are visible. These defences marked the north-western corner of the Roman defences for the settlement, although the London Wall was rebuilt in the medieval period. The visible parts of the tower are original and only survived because it was buried under rubbish and waste soil from the nearby churchyard. It was uncovered

A London Wall bastion at the Barbican Estate.

when the Barbican Estate was constructed, and the extent of the surviving remains were revealed.

Directions & Accessibility: Walking around any part of the Barbican Estate on the south side, and it is difficult to miss the London Wall and the various other remains. The ruins are accessible by following the path on the north side of Monkwell Square, through the Barbican Estate, and which leads past the back of Barber-Surgeons' Hall (see separate entry). Access into the estate itself is restricted, but the best views of the Roman tower and remains can be seen from outside of St Giles, Cripplegate. The quickest route to the church is from the north-eastern corner of Monkswell Square.

20 | Barber-Surgeons' Hall
London Wall Walk 16 and 17
London Wall | Tower | No Facilities | Barbican
Monkwell Square, Wood Street | EC2Y 5BL | TQ 323 816 | cats.snail.sleeps
www.barber-surgeonshall.com

Located close to the Barbican Estate (see previous entry), and in the shadow of the former Museum of London building at Barbican House, there are some lengthy sections

The Physic Garden within the London Wall remains at the Barber-Surgeons' Hall.

of London Wall and various bastion remains, as well as the recreated Physic Garden here. Along with the London Wall, this section also incorporates the north and west walls of the Cripplegate fort, two internal turrets, four bastions and the more visible medieval city walls. Not all of these remains are visible above ground, but what can be seen is impressive, although neglected in places. Some sections have been reconstructed, such as bastion 12, which is in the north-west corner and was reconstructed in 1900; beneath the bastion is a turret which belongs to the Roman fort. The Barber-Surgeons' Hall is located on top of the fort and originally incorporated part of the Wall into its structure, although this section was severely damaged during the Great Fire of London, and other parts of the building destroyed in bombing raids during the Second World War.

Directions & Accessibility: There are quite a few upstanding remains to be seen in this area, although most of what is visible is either medieval or reconstructed, but it is worth following the line of the Wall and exploring all the nooks and crannies. The area around the Barber-Surgeons' Hall is freely accessible, and it is also possible to visit the adjacent Physic Garden which grows in the shadow of one of the bastions. The Hall itself can only be visited on open days. There are paths around the Wall, although there are a few steps within the garden. At the time of writing, it was possible to access this part of the Wall from the southern end, next to the Museum of London. However, this site is due to undergo redevelopment as the Museum of London is moving to Billingsgate. The site can also be accessed by following the path from the Barbican/St Giles Cripplegate section of the Wall.

21 | Museum of London
Closed | Barbican
150 London Wall | EC2Y 5HN | TQ 322 816 | allows.flesh.list
www.museumoflondon.org.uk/museum-london

The Museum of London is a wonderful place. Full of exhibits and objects telling the story of London, from pre-Roman times until the modern day. It is renowned for its collection of Roman objects, which vary from the usual coins and pottery, to shoes, slave chains and even underwear. However, after forty-five years literally on top of the London Wall, the Museum of London has closed as it is moving to a larger site at Smithfield, which is due to open in 2026. Housed in the old Smithfield General Market buildings, the new museum will be larger than its predecessor, be much more accessible and have considerably more space to display items and host temporary exhibitions. The Roman collections will be key to this, and the museum promises great things for telling the story of Londinium. Although the London Wall site has closed, the Museum of London Docklands (see separate entry) remains open and is worth making time to see, despite a lack of information on the Thames in Roman times.

Directions & Accessibility: The Museum of London is closed as it is relocating to Smithfield General Market. There are nearby remains of the London Wall and various bastions located mainly to the east and south of the old museum building at London Wall (see the Barber-Surgeons' Hall entry).

22 | Bastion House (Former Museum of London) | City Wall and Medieval Tower
London Wall Walk 18
Remains | London Wall | Gate | No Facilities | St Paul's
140 London Wall | EC2Y 5AB | TQ 322 815 | hired.acute.knee

Discovered during construction of the London Wall road in 1959, this section of the Roman and medieval London Wall was also originally part of the Cripplegate fort defences. During excavations, archaeologists found that this section of the London Wall had been physically added to the fort wall to make it wider and thicker.

Directions & Accessibility: The area is fairly accessible, although on an incline (or steps) down to the ground level where the remains are. There are walkways in the area, crossing over London Wall road and these can give a good view of the bastions and Wall. Most of the walkways are accessible and signposted. There are no remains to be seen by Bastion House, but within the adjacent London Wall Car Park (see separate entry) is a section of the Wall.

23 | Noble Street Garden
London Wall Walk 19
Remains | Fort | London Wall | No Facilities | St Paul's
No. 3 Noble Street | EC2V 7JU | TQ 322 814 | behind.crowd.scenes

Part of the Cripplegate fort wall surrounded by ruins within Noble Street Garden.

In between tower blocks and offices lies this surprising and somewhat neglected collection of Roman, medieval and nineteenth-century remains within Noble Street Garden. Visible from street level, the remains include a section of London Wall, standing at 4.5 metres high. While there are Roman foundations, the majority of it is medieval. In front of the main section of London Wall are the foundations of the defensive walls of the Cripplegate fort, which was constructed first. When the London Wall was built, the fort wall was incorporated into the plan; the London Wall is tacked on behind the fort wall. There are two Roman turrets, including the corner tower of the fort, along with a bastion at the south-west end of the section. The Roman layers are quite distinct from the medieval stonework, which sits above the earlier layers. Some of the more visible remains in the Gardens actually belong to buildings built between the eighteenth and twentieth centuries and which were bomb damaged in the Second World War.

Directions & Accessibility: Located at the northern end of Noble Street, on the east side, the remains are visible from an accessible street-level walkway, which also has interpretation panels. It is not possible to wander around these remains.

24 | Goldsmiths' Hall
Temple | No Facilities | St Paul's
Foster Lane | EC2V 6BN | TQ 322 813 | shop.hunt.frock
www.thegoldsmiths.co.uk

An example of a relatively nondescript nineteenth-century livery hall, which is home to the Worshipful Company of Goldsmiths. Initially constructed in 1830, workers uncovered a Roman altar to the goddess Diana around 4.5 metres below street level. Several pieces of Roman masonry were also discovered and archaeologists have speculated that this may have originally been the site of a Roman temple.

Directions & Accessibility: There are no Roman remains to be seen here, and the hall can only be visited on open days. Accessibility is limited due to the historic nature of the building.

25 | Aldermanbury
Fort | Gate | No Facilities | St Paul's & Moorgate
Aldermanbury, Cheap | EC2V 7RF | TQ 324 813 | shelf.mirror.talked

The walls of the Cripplegate Roman fort run almost parallel with the northern half of Aldermanbury, where part of the east gate of the fort was located underneath the road (TQ 324 813). Underneath the top end of the lower half of Aldermanbury, and opposite the Guildhall Library (TQ 324 814), the south-east corner turret of the fort has been located.

Directions & Accessibility: Neither of the aforementioned features are marked on the ground, and there are no visible remains to be seen at this location.

26 | Guildhall and Guildhall Yard
Remains | Amphitheatre | Museum | Bank
Guildhall Yard | EC2V 5AE | TQ 324 813 | luxury.money.darker
www.cityoflondon.gov.uk/things-to-do/attractions-museums-entertainment/londons-roman-amphitheatre

Most Roman towns and cities across the empire would have had an amphitheatre – a place where everyone came together to celebrate festivals and enjoy sporting entertainment, some of it quite brutal and involving animals. Although there are relatively few examples of amphitheatres in Britain, London has one of the most impressive and largest examples underneath Guildhall Yard. Initially discovered in 1951, when a small trench led to the discovery of a substantial Roman wall, it was not until the late 1980s that the site was extensively excavated. There had been some

The Guildhall.

previous excavations in the area, but it wasn't until the construction of the Guildhall Art Gallery that a full investigation could be undertaken. That work revealed the size and extent of the amphitheatre, and beneath it was an older, large timber structure built in the mid- to late first century. Archaeologists believe it was an early, wooden amphitheatre which was demolished to make way for the later stone version which was much bigger and more impressive. Dating evidence uncovered during the excavations suggested that the new amphitheatre was constructed between the early and middle of the second century, and eventually abandoned 200 years later when rubbish was dumped inside of the internal rooms, while the stonework was removed for use in the construction of other buildings.

The amphitheatre is elliptical, 105 metres long and 85 metres wide. Within the basement of the Guildhall Art Gallery are the surviving remains of the amphitheatre. On display is an outer wall, behind which would have been the banks of seating for spectators. An inner wall originally encircled the arena, within which the entertainment or sport would have taken place. The eastern entrance to the arena can also be seen, and on either side of this are two small rooms or chambers which archaeologists have speculated were either changing rooms or shrines to various gods. Outside, in Guildhall Yard, the elliptical route of the outer wall of the amphitheatre is marked in dark stone.

Directions & Accessibility: The Guildhall Art Gallery can be found on the eastern side of Guildhall Yard. There is free access to the Gallery, and visitors can wander around the remains in the basement. There are also guided tours focussing on the amphitheatre.

27 | Ironmonger Lane
Remains | Mosaic | No Facilities | Bank
No. 11 Ironmonger Lane | EC2V 8EY | TQ 325 812 | paused.demand.title

During post-war rebuilding at No. 11 Ironmonger Lane, traces of ancient walls were discovered, along with a large piece of third-century mosaic which had an intricate, geometrical pattern, while below this were pieces of mid-second century pottery. The mosaic still survives in the basement of No. 11, beneath a glass floor. Further excavations in the 1980s uncovered a building dating to the first century, along with a section of road and a horse skeleton dating to the early medieval period.

Halfway along the street are a set of gates marking the entrance into the old churchyard of St Martin Pomary, and behind this is the tower of St Olave which originally belonged to the church of the same name, but this was demolished in 1892. During its demolition more Roman stonework was discovered within its walls.

Directions & Accessibility: The mosaic is in the basement of No. 11 Ironmonger Lane, which is occupied by a private company, and therefore there is no access to the remains.

No. 11 Ironmonger Lane.

28 | Bank of England Museum
Remains | Mosaics | Museum | Toilets | Bank
Bartholomew Lane | EC2R 8AH | TQ 327 812 | again.saints.funny
www.bankofengland.co.uk/museum

You might not think that the Bank of England Museum would be home to Roman remains, but during construction of the building in the 1920s, workers dug down 15 metres deep to create the space needed for the gold vaults. Digging through the old layers of Londinium, they came across a huge stash of artefacts and remains. Many of these items are now in the collection of the museum and can be seen on display. They include a huge range of everyday items such as pottery, shoes, writing tablets and other items from daily life in Londinium.

   Decorative mosaic floors were also discovered, with the first being uncovered by Sir John Soane (who also founded the nearby museum named after himself), and which are now on display in the British Museum. Another magnificent mosaic was discovered later and although it had been damaged by the oak piles used to underpin the original museum building in the early nineteenth century, it was saved and is now on display in the museum.

Directions & Accessibility: The Bank of England looms over Threadneedle Street and the surrounding area. However, the museum entrance is on Bartholomew Lane, to the east of the Bank, and off Threadneedle Street. There are some steps to access the museum, but there are ramps and an accessible lift. More details can be found on their website.

29 | Aldersgate
London Wall Walk 21
London Wall | City Gate | No Facilities | St Paul's
EC1A 4ER | TQ 321 814 | matter.dairy.glue

Aldersgate is the location of another gateway through the Roman city walls. It was still in use in the early medieval period when it was known as Ealdred's Gate, before being rebuilt in the seventeenth century and then demolished in 1761. Development work in the nineteenth century uncovered the foundations of the London Wall, which were 3 metres thick at the base, tapering to almost 2 metres at the top, while being 3 metres high. However, it in unclear how much of this was originally built by the Romans and how much resulted from its continuing use in the medieval period. Just over 3 metres from the Wall was the defensive ditch, which measured almost 4.5 metres deep, with the bottom being over 10.5 metres wide. There was also some evidence for a wooden bridge crossing the ditch.

Directions & Accessibility: There are no remains to be seen in this location.

30 | St Botolph-without-Bishopgate Church
London Wall Walk 9
London Wall | City Gate | No Facilities | St Paul's
Bishopsgate | EC1A 4EU | TQ 321 815 | kick.logo.limes

The line of the London Wall marked the edge of the boundary of St Botolph's churchyard, running parallel with Wormwood Street. Over the centuries, buildings were built up against the Wall, and eventually it was subsumed into the structure of these. In the early eighteenth century, during the rebuilding of the church, a Roman tomb was uncovered with two skeletons buried within, although these are not on display.

Directions & Accessibility: There are no Roman remains to be seen at this location, although the church can be visited.

31 | Postman's Park (King Edward Street)
Remains | London Wall | No Facilities | St Paul's
King Edward Street/St Martin's Le Grand | EC1A 7BT | TQ 320 814 | delay.blog.extend

Postman's Park was created on the former burial ground of St Botolph's, Aldersgate, in 1880, and grew to incorporate a number of adjacent burial grounds. While the

Postman's Park.

London Wall survives in the area for as long as 40 metres, it remains buried beneath the ground. Within the southern boundary of the park there is a further stretch of London Wall embedded in the foundations of the former General Post Office (GPO) building, now offices on the south side of the park. The foundations are not visible from within the park.

There are other interesting features to see in the park; on the west side is the Memorial to Heroic Self-Sacrifice, a collection of ceramic tablets which commemorates ordinary people who died saving others. There are also collections of surviving grave markers from the earlier burial grounds which can be glimpsed in the undergrowth, particularly near the fountain.

Directions & Accessibility: Accessed from several points, in particular St Martin's Le Grand, the park sits in between the old GPO building and the London City Presbyterian

Church, itself worth a visit. The foundations of the London Wall are visible in a space between the edge of the park and the building, but unfortunately cannot really be seen from the park and are not otherwise accessible to the public.

32 | Bank of America Financial Centre
Remains | London Wall | Bastion | No Facilities | St Paul's
King Edward Street | EC1A 1HQ | TQ 320 814 | props.robot.normal

Early in the early twentieth century, during construction of the nearby GPO building, a section of London Wall and medieval bastion were uncovered with the remains eventually preserved within the GPO building, although access for visitors was not permitted. Fast forward to the twenty-first century, and the site has been further redeveloped, and the remains put on display. At the time of writing, the building containing the Roman Wall is due to be sold and refurbished, but the remains should continue to be accessible. Previously, the owners had done an excellent job of presenting this hidden section of the Wall, beneath a financial powerhouse, and it is hoped that the new owners continue to do the same.

Interestingly, when the GPO building was still in use as a post office, an underground mail train ran beneath the streets of London, taking post from Paddington to Whitechapel, with one station in between being the building at King Edward Street. Although the mail train ceased operating in 2003, parts of the tunnels can be explored from the Postal Museum at Mount Pleasant.

Directions & Accessibility: At the time of writing, the site is undergoing renovation. Previously, the site was only accessible through the Bank of America Financial Centre, with access times limited to office hours. However, the refurbished building may have different access arrangements.

33 | Old Bailey (Central Criminal Courts)
Remains | London Wall | No Facilities | City Thameslink
Old Bailey | EC4M 7EH | TQ 318 813 | just.assets.ears

The London Wall turns up in the strangest of places, with a 7-metre section, standing to 1.5 metres high, found in the basement of the Central Criminal Court, otherwise known as the Old Bailey, which itself is partially built on the site of the infamous Newgate Prison. Discovered during building work on the site, the foundations and bottom courses of the Roman wall survive, with additional sections of Wall surviving nearby, although these are buried and not visible.

Directions & Accessibility: Located on the corner of Old Bailey and Newgate Street, the imposing Victorian Central Criminal Courts building, with its distinctive dome, cannot be missed. The section of London Wall in the basement of the Old Bailey is not accessible to visitors.

The Old Bailey.

34 | Amen Court
Remains | London Wall | No Facilities | City Thameslink
EC4M 7NG | TQ 318 812 | wiring.pilots.answer

Supposedly built by famed architect Sir Christopher Wren, the man who led the rebuilding of many churches and other buildings after the devastation of the Great Fire, Amen Court is home to a small row of seventeenth-century terraced houses. Hidden away in the shadow of St Paul's Cathedral, there is a small, tranquil garden at the western end of the court. At the far end of this is an old wall which separates Amen Court from the rest of the world, and, at one time, separated the residents from the prisoners' graveyard for Newgate Prison. The lower levels of the boundary originally formed part of the London Wall, and Roman masonry can clearly be seen in the bottom.

Directions & Accessibility: Amen Court is owned by St Paul's Cathedral, and is not accessible to the public without prior permission from the Dean and Chapter.

35 | Ludgate Hill
Wall | No Facilities | City Thameslink
EC4M 7JN | TQ 317 811 | packet.panels.roses

Numerous Roman discoveries have been made in the Ludgate area, which was one of the busiest entrances into Londinium. There is even evidence to suggest that the road from Ludgate Hill to Hammersmith was originally a prehistoric trackway, later 'upgraded' to become a major Roman thoroughfare.

Local discoveries include a possible aqueduct in Ludgate Square, and a large tombstone of a soldier which was found in 1669 in the grounds of nearby church,

Ludgate Hill.

St Martin, Ludgate. Another tombstone found at Ludgate Hill offers an interesting insight into the lives of Romans and their slaves as the inscription reads, 'In memory of Claudia Martina, aged 19. Set up by Anoncletus, slave of the province, to his most devoted wife. She lies here.'

Directions & Accessibility: There are no Roman remains to be seen in this location.

36 | St Bride's Church
Remains | Road | No Facilities | City Thameslink
Fleet Street | EC4Y 8AU | TQ 315 811 | buyers.expect.dinner
www.stbrides.com

Perhaps best known for being the 'church of journalists' and for its distinctive layered spire, at 69 metres tall St Bride's is the second tallest church designed by Sir Christopher Wren in the aftermath of the Great Fire (only St Paul's Cathedral is taller). Believed to

St Bride's Church, Fleet Street.

date back to the early medieval period, the oldest remains can be found beneath the church, dating to Roman times. The church was bombed in the 1940s, and subsequent excavation revealed two sections of tessellated or mosaic-style Roman floors. Located at the far end of the undercroft space, which also houses a museum of finds from the site, the mosaics are hidden behind a medieval wall but visible as reflections in a pair of mirrors. The floorings are assumed to come from a suburban villa which was located on the hillside now occupied by the church and overlooking the valley of the River Fleet. Excavations also revealed a particularly wide Roman ditch, 4.5 to 5.5 metres, which was much wider than the defensive ditch surrounding the city. The purpose and dating of the ditch remains a mystery. Look out for the Roman artefacts on display in the undercroft.

Besides Roman floors, there is much else to see in St Bride's. In the north-east of the church is the Journalists' Altar, which was where vigils were held for John McCarthy when he was held hostage in Beirut. There is also a memorial to Polly Nichols, one of the early victims of Jack the Ripper, who was married in the church in 1864. There is a medieval chapel which is worth seeking out, and a Victorian iron casket (visible in the crypt) that was used to secure corpses to prevent them being stolen by body snatchers. A word of warning: the crypt also contains a charnel house, a place where bones and skulls recovered from the burial ground are stored. This can be seen on tours of the church.

Directions & Accessibility: St Bride's is slightly hidden away, and can be found to the west of the intersection of Fleet Street and New Bridge Street. From that junction, head west and take the first left on the south pavement, at St Bride's Avenue, and the church is just ahead. It is not visible from Fleet Street. The main church is accessible, but access to the crypt is down several steps, and the floor is uneven. The website has more information on accessibility.

City of London: South

Though the River Thames borders the southern half of the City of London, it did not stop Rome's citizens, merchants and traders from crossing the waterway and establishing themselves in what is now Southwark. To the north of the Thames, Londinium continued to thrive, and a world of Roman remains lies buried beneath the streets.

37 | Blackfriars
Wreck | No Facilities | Blackfriars
Paul's Walk | EC4V 3DB | TQ 317 808 | forum.risen.foal

During construction of a river wall at Blackfriars in 1962, workers discovered the remains of a Roman ship which was 18 metres long and just under 3 metres wide. When it was uncovered stones were found in the hull, leading to speculation that it

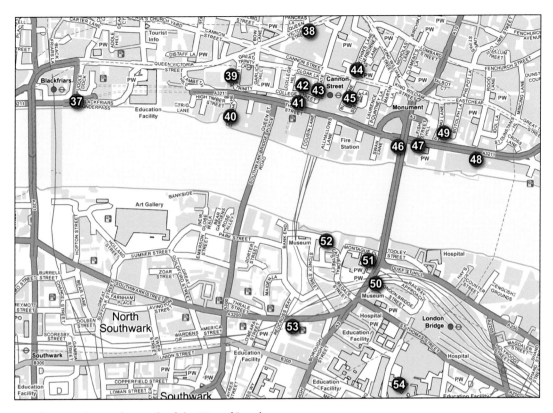

Roman sites to the south of the City of London.

was a cargo ship transporting building stone when it sank. Archaeologists also found a rough millstone, which has led some to suggest that the ship may have previously transported such a cargo from either northern England or Belgium. A coin found wedged in the mast-step (probably as a good-luck offering), was minted around CE 79, while artefacts found with the boat suggest it was still being used around CE 150. However, dendrochronological analysis of wooden planks from the wreck indicated that the trees these came from were felled sometime between CE 130 and 175. This has led archaeologists to speculate that the boat was probably in use in the middle of the second century before sinking shortly afterwards. The cause of its demise is unknown, but given it was found near a possible quay, some suggest that the vessel was involved in a collision with another ship, leading to its loss.

Directions & Accessibility: There are no remains to be seen at Blackfriars, although a model of the hull is in the collection of the Science Museum.

38 | London Mithraeum
Remains | Temple | No Facilities | Mansion House
No. 12 Walbrook | EC4N 8AA | TQ 325 810 | lands.sports.look
www.londonmithraeum.com

One of London's most impressive (and free) visitor attractions, the Roman *mithraeum* is a multi-sensory experience of what life may have been like in this temple. At the heart of Mithraism is the worship of the god Mithras, and it is a religion which is closely associated with the Roman military in the second and third centuries. Such temples, known as *mithraeum,* are often located underground, or in some instances within a partially sunken chamber, to give the impression of being subterranean. Such temples are found across the empire, although are rare in Britain.

The London *mithraeum* was found in 1954 ahead of the construction of Bucklesbury House at No. 248 Walbrook. Just as excavations were ending, the marble head of a statue of Mithras was uncovered and after some lobbying, the excavations continued and most of the temple site was uncovered. Like most *mithraeum*, the London one was also subterranean with worshippers descending into a chamber, similar to a church, with a central nave with seven columns on each side and an apse at one end, where the altars to the gods were kept. Evidence from the London excavations has indicated that the temple was initially constructed in the late second or early third centuries.

Given the amount of public interest in the original 1950s excavations, the remains of the temple were put on display to the public, although for many years this was in a different location (Queen Victoria Street) from where it was discovered. Eventually, the remains were removed in 2011 and moved closer to the original site when Bloomberg began work on their new building. As part of planning permission for the new building, Bloomberg were required to restore the remains and make them publicly accessible, and they have done an amazing job. Descending below street level, there is an opportunity to see some of the finds uncovered during the original excavations, as well as the hundreds recovered during construction of the new building. There is a museum exhibition space, telling visitors about the cult, before they are taken into the heart of the *mithraeum* and given the opportunity to visualise, hear and feel what it would have been like to be a worshipper of Mithras, almost 2,000 years ago. During construction of the new building, archaeologists also discovered a large cache of writing tablets, including the earliest known written reference to Londinium. The tablets offer a special insight into the daily lives of those living in Roman London and are fascinating. Some of them are on display at the *mithraeum*, while others will be on display in the new Museum of London.

Directions & Accessibility: Located next to the Walbrook entrance to Bank station, the Mithraeum is well signposted and hard to miss. Entered from street level, the Mithraeum space is fully accessible, with lift access down to the temple. There are the remains of the temple to be seen, but there is also a light and projection performance to help visitors experience the life of a Mithraic worshiper. During performances, the space is in darkness and some visitors may find this claustrophobic. Some visitors with mobility issues may wish to consult the venue or check the website in advance of visiting.

39 | Huggin Hill
Remains | Baths | No Facilities | Mansion House
EC4V 2AD | TQ 322 808 | cling.dream.select

In the nineteenth and early twentieth centuries, evidence of Roman buildings in the Huggin Hill area had been revealed through sewer construction and other developments. This included a section of building wall, 1.5 metres thick and running for 11 metres, suggesting something substantial was buried here. In the 1960s and again in the 1980s, extensive excavation took place in this area, revealing a sizeable bathhouse complex at Huggin Hill. Evidence from the site suggests that construction began in the late first century and was further developed in the second, before finally being abandoned in the third century. At some point, the bathhouse may have stretched for as long as 75 metres along the river front.

The site has not been fully excavated, but there are at least seven main rooms, including the usual cold, warm and hot rooms. Archaeologists have debated whether or not the buildings were public baths or a public building or palace with a bath complex attached. Either way, the remains survive to a height of just over 3 metres and are some of the highest standing, visible Roman remains in London.

Directions & Accessibility: The original site of the baths is located under Upper Thames Street and surrounding area, with a large part of the complex beneath the surrounding office blocks. However, it is worth visiting Cleary Garden (EC1A 7BA | wie.taxi.door) which is constructed on part of the site, and has Roman influences in its design. The garden offers a spot of tranquillity in the busy city. Within the garden are remains of cellars and fragments of buildings destroyed in the Blitz. In amongst some of the undergrowth, some of the Roman wall is visible, although the vegetation makes it difficult to see. Accessibility is partially limited within the garden due to steps.

40 | Queenhithe Dock | Smith's Wharf
Wharf | No Facilities | Mansion House
Queenhithe | EC4V 3EH | TQ 322 807 | supporter.free.sorry

Located on the bank of the River Thames by Southwark Bridge, Queenhithe Dock is a small and unassuming inlet on the waterfront, but it has a long and important history. Reputed to be the site where Alfred the Great re-established London in 886, Queenhithe was an active wharf area in Roman times, and continued in use into the early medieval period, with evidence of later occupation in the twelfth and fourteenth centuries. It was only in the nineteenth century that the Queenhithe went out of use when the adjacent Smith's Wharf was constructed. Archaeological evidence from the area around Queenhithe has shown that there was heavy occupation of the area in Roman times, with a series of waterfront buildings overlooking the river. On the eastern side of the walkway, overlooking the dock, is the Queenhithe Mosaic, a 30-metre-long artwork which tells the story of London, beginning with the Romans.

The shoreline at Queenhithe dock.

Directions & Accessibility: Queenhithe and Smith's Wharf are best accessed from Upper Thames Street. The lane running down to Queenhithe is next to the Thames Court building, where a modern footbridge over Upper Thames Street ends. The Queenhithe Mosaic is on the right, while a plaque marking King Alfred's return to London is ahead. Alternatively, the Thames Path follows the waterfront and passes Queenhithe.

41 | Innholders' Hall
Waterfront | No Facilities | Cannon Street
No. 30 College Street | EC4R 2RH | TQ 325 808 | puff.radio.guises
www.innholders.org.uk

Belonging to the Worshipful Company of Innholders, which has its origins in the sixteenth century and still has links to the hospitality trade, Innholders' Hall has been altered several times and survived the Blitz. Located on the Thames waterfront, it is no surprise that Roman foundations were discovered beneath the Hall, and which belong to riverside buildings of the time.

Directions & Accessibility: There are no remains to be seen at this location, and there is no public access to the Hall.

42 | Skinners' Hall
Waterfront | No Facilities | Cannon Street
No. 8 Dowgate Hill | EC4R 2SP | TQ 325 808 | just.nets.loose
www.skinnershall.com

For 700 years, Skinners' Hall has been home to the Worshipful Company of Skinners, although the current hall dates to the seventeenth century. The Hall is located on the site of the so called Roman Governor's Palace. Excavations nearby have led to the discovery of a Roman well, along with medieval and later finds. It is likely that there is a wealth of archaeological remains beneath Skinners' Hall.

Directions & Accessibility: There are no Roman remains to be seen at this location, and at the time of writing the Hall is undergoing a significant restoration and will be reopened from 2024 and may be accessible to visitors.

43 | Dyers' Hall
Mosaic | No Facilities | Cannon Street
Nos 11–13 Dowgate Hill | EC4R 2SU | TQ 325 808 | pencil.spare.snow
www.dyerscompany.co.uk

In the nineteenth century, during building work on the site of Dyers' Hall, a mosaic was uncovered 5 metres below street level, along with other artefacts such as pottery. The mosaic is likely to have belonged to a grand building overlooking the water front, although it could also be linked to the nearby so-called Governor's Palace. More recently, further development work within the Hall has uncovered further evidence of Roman activity at the site.

Directions & Accessibility: There are no remains to be seen at this location, and it is not currently possible to visit the Hall.

44 | The London Stone
Remains | Stone | No Facilities | Cannon Street
No. 111 Cannon Street | EC4N 5AD | TQ 326 809 | faced.intro.hiding

Possibly one of the most famous relics of Roman London, the stone has a chequered history, and despite the legend that disaster should fall on London should it be moved, it has been relocated on a number of occasions. It is also said to be the point that all distances in Roman Britain were measured from, although this is an urban legend. Formed out of a larger block of limestone, the London Stone may have its origins in the Roman period, although there is no definitive evidence that it dates to the period. It was mentioned in various early medieval texts, and by the 1740s, it was on Candlewick Street (now Cannon Street), but was moved when the road was widened. There is some speculation that the rest of the stone still lies somewhere. By the sixteenth century, the stone had become a bit of a tourist attraction, and is noted in a poem on the sights of London. In 1742, the stone was moved to beside St Swithin's Church, and over the next eighty years moved to various places within the church grounds. After the destruction of St Swithin's in the Blitz, the site was redeveloped (becoming No. 111 Cannon Street), and the stone was housed in a niche of the building. For a time, the building became a newsagents, and the stone was hidden behind magazine racks.

The London Stone, Canon Street.

It was Sir Christopher Wren, in 1750, who put forward the argument that as the stone was found next to a Roman road, and as there were numerous mosaics found nearby, it must have come from a nearby Roman building. Some have jumped on this argument, suggesting that the building may have been the nearby Governor's Palace (see separate entry). In 2018, the stone was relocated back to Cannon Street, where it now sits on a stone plinth behind protective glass.

Directions & Accessibility: Located on the north side of Cannon Street, almost opposite the station entrance and by a set of traffic lights, the London Stone is set in an ornate glass and stone enclosure built into the wall of an office block. Access to the area is good.

45 | Governor's Palace
Palace | No Facilities | Cannon Street
Cannon Street/Upper Thames Street | EC4R 0AN | TQ 326 808 | funny.dads.unity

Development of the waterfront area of Central London has revealed many Roman treasures and buildings which have been hidden, and many would have gone unnoticed if it had not had been for such work. Sometimes this has been instigated because of damage during events such as the Great Fire of London in 1666, bombing during the Blitz in the Second World War or major civil improvements. The site of the Governor's Palace is one such location, with evidence for a Roman structure coming to light on several occasions; for example, during rebuilding work in the aftermath of the Great Fire, during the installation of sewers in the 1840s and when Cannon Street station was built in 1868.

Located in the block surrounded by Cannon Street on the north, Cannon Bridge and Upper Thames Street in the south, Dowgate Hill and Laurence Poutney Lane in the east and west, the Governor's Palace was a substantial and important building in Roman London. Initially occupied in the late first century, it was only abandoned around CE 270, which led to the construction of minor buildings on the site. In its heyday, the building was surrounded by large walls, had open-air courtyards and internally had grand rooms with architectural features such as apses, all indicating that this was an important building which was established as a sign of wealth and power. It was designed to impress both visitors and ordinary citizens of Londinium. The size and impressive architectural features have led to the conclusion that the building's occupants were important members of Roman society, more than likely the Governor of Roman Britain and his retinue.

The palace was not the first building on the site. Archaeologists have found evidence for a goldsmith's workshop in one corner and an early timber building, possibly associated with the military, on another part of the site, indicating that this had been a part of Roman London which had been occupied for a long time.

Directions & Accessibility: There are no remains of the palace to be seen in this location.

46 | Fishmongers' Hall
Palace | No Facilities | Monument
London Bridge | EC4R 9EL | TQ 328 806 | icons.vouch.cafe
www.fishmongers.org.uk

Home to the Worshipful Company of Fishmongers, the nineteenth-century livery hall is the latest in a long line of such buildings stretching back as far as the fifteenth century, with the earliest recorded at the beginning of the fourteenth century. Located on waterfront of the River Thames, the site has important Roman connections as it lies on the main second-century wharf of Londinium. This was first recorded in the mid-1970s when the adjacent Seal House was demolished, revealing horizontal timbers and piles. A little to the west of Fishmongers' Hall lies the Roman Governor's Palace complex, demonstrating the importance of waterfront locations in Londinium.

Directions & Accessibility: There are no remains to be seen at this location, and it is not currently possible to visit the Hall.

47 | Church of St Magnus the Martyr
Remains | Bridge | No Facilities | Monument
Lower Thames Street | EC3R 6DN | TQ 329 806 | assure.ties.kind
www.stmagnusmartyr.org.uk

The Church of St Magnus the Martyr is one of the most spectacular and ornate of all the old churches in London. Apparently, it was the most expensive and opulent of the churches designed by Sir Christopher Wren in the aftermath of the Great Fire of London. The church itself is built next to the original approach road onto Old London Bridge, which spanned the Thames between here and Southwark on the opposite bank. The church had stood in this position since 1176, but when Old London Bridge was widened in the 1760s, the church and grounds were in the way, so the both building and churchyard were drastically altered, with the latter being almost completely obliterated.

In 1931, during construction work nearby, a timber pile was uncovered and was assumed to be from a Roman waterside structure. Indeed, the accompanying plaque states that the pile dates to CE 75 and was recovered from a wharf. Although the dating of the timber is guesswork, it is nonetheless an interesting curio. The timber can be found attached to the wall of the external porch of the church, on its western side. While here, it is worth taking a quick look inside the church, especially to see the impressive model of Old London Bridge, which spanned the river with its arches and numerous buildings.

Directions & Accessibility: Located on the south side of Lower Thames Street, close to where new London Bridge crosses over it, the Church of St Magnus the Martyr is unmistakably austere. The timber is inside the porch, beneath the bell tower on the

Wood from a Roman wharf on display outside the Church of St Magnus the Martyr.

west side of building. The timber is tucked away and not obvious. The building has some restrictive access.

48 | Billingsgate | Former Coal Exchange
Remains | Bathhouse | No Facilities | Monument
No. 101 Lower Thames Street | EC3R 6EA | TQ 331 806 | casual.works.gender
www.cityoflondon.gov.uk/things-to-do/attractions-museums-entertainment/
billingsgate-bathhouse

Beneath the streets of the Square Mile lies some of the most impressive remains from Roman London, the Billingsgate Roman House and Baths. Initially discovered during development work in the 1840s, and further revealed during excavations in the late 1960s and early 1970s, the remains belong to a second-century house or inn (*mansio*) which overlooked the Thames. The original owners had some wealth given the prime location and because there was a *hypocaust* in the east wing. In the third century, a small bathhouse was added to the main building, and this had a suite of rooms for bathers, including a cold room (*frigidarium*), warm room (*tepidarium*) and a hot room (*caldarium*). The buildings seem to have lasted for several hundred years, before eventually being abandoned in the mid-fifth century.

Directions & Accessibility: Although Billingsgate is on the south side of Upper Thames Street, the entrance is via an office block on the north side and is clearly marked. Booking is required for visiting the site, with tours regularly taking place at weekends and bookable through the website. As the site is underground, access is limited and there are steps down to the site.

49 | Pudding Lane
Bridge | No Facilities | Monument
Pudding Lane | EC3R 8AB | TQ 329 807 | cargo.allows.pits

Memorial to the Great Fire of London, Pudding Lane.

A stone structure found during works at Pudding Lane has been identified as being the abutment or foundations of one of the earliest Roman bridges to cross the River Thames. Information on the Roman bridges across the river is vague, but it is thought that the first bridge was constructed around the middle of the first century but was soon replaced towards the end of that period. The abutment and bridge seem to have gone out of use a short time later as it was covered over by a quay around CE 120. A new bridge was then built, slightly further to the east, possibly of stone.

Directions & Accessibility: There are no visible remains to be seen at this location.

50 | Borough High Street

Bathhouse | No Facilities | London Bridge
SE1 9SF | TQ 327 802 | about.forgot.post

Originally part of the Roman road network, Borough High Street would have connected to the road linking Londinium and Chichester (where it becomes Newington Causeway). Many impressive Roman secrets have come to light in the Southwark area. In the 1970s, archaeologists working in the vicinity of Nos 207–211 Borough High Street uncovered a series of timber buildings dating to the Roman period. Occupied from the first century to the middle of the second, the site then appears to have been abandoned until the construction of stone buildings in the late third to mid-fourth centuries. Nearby, during the construction of part of St Thomas' Hospital, a Roman floor surface comprising red *tesserae* was discovered.

Although there have been various Roman discoveries in and around Borough High Street, one of the most notable was revealed at the beginning of the twenty-first century, in advance of improvements to the rail network. In 2011, excavations began on a piece of land at the north end of Borough High Street, where it meets London Bridge Street. In the Roman period, this part of Borough High Street would have been an island in the Thames, and close to the waterline and the Roman bridgehead. The excavations revealed that there was some indication, albeit slight, of pre-Roman activity on the site, but it was not until the Romans arrived that the site became more extensively used. At one end, archaeologists uncovered evidence of industrial workings which lasted until the early part of the second century, while at the other were signs of domestic activity. On the north side, archaeologists uncovered a bathhouse, which was initially built in the second century. There was a large, circular room, about 5 metres in diameter, which appears to have been used as the *laconicum*, a Roman type of sauna. This room lasted until the late second century when it was abandoned and used as a rubbish dump. Additional rooms on the north-eastern side of the site were excavated, but not enough of the building was cleared to figure out what the rooms were used for, although they were refurbished at some point. Despite the building being either a public bathhouse or belonging to someone wealthy, the complex was abandoned by the fourth century and the stones from the buildings reused elsewhere.

Directions & Accessibility: There are no Roman remains to be seen at Borough High Street.

51 | Southwark Cathedral
Remains | Road | No Facilities | London Bridge
London Bridge | SE1 9DA | TQ 327 803 | emerge.card.cabin
www.cathedral.southwark.anglican.org

Despite the growth of Londinium on the northern bank of the Thames, it did not stop people flocking across the river to live and work, much as happens today. The area around Southwark, particularly the cathedral, has thrown up lots of evidence of early activity and occupation. Large parts of Southwark's ancient history emerged when the railways were driven through the wharves and warehouses in the nineteenth century, but also more recently as the area grows and is redeveloped. Such works have not only highlighted the importance of the south side of the river in Roman times, but the evidence indicates that people were crossing the Thames as early as the first century, almost as soon as Londinium was established.

Within the cathedral precinct, there have been numerous Roman finds, some recorded as early as 1825, and these include at least one Roman burial. Work in the cathedral crypt, during the late 1970s, revealed evidence of a timber-well

Southwark Cathedral.

dating to the second century, but which was filled with rubbish when it went out of use. Another well was then dug nearby in the third century, and refurbished less than 100 years later, before it too was abandoned. The site yielded evidence of first-century timber buildings which were eventually demolished and do not appear to have been replaced in later centuries as it became a dumping ground for masonry and fragments of funerary monuments.

In 1999, subsequent archaeological works in and around the cathedral uncovered more Roman remains, including sections of road, along with evidence for buildings on either side of it. There were fragments of painted wall plaster found among the rubble of demolished buildings, indicating that there may have been some wealthy owners living in this area. Archaeological evidence indicates these buildings were in use from the mid-first century until the late second or early third centuries.

At one point, the finds from the 1977 excavations were on display at the Cuming Museum, although this has now been incorporated into the Southwark Heritage Centre and Walworth Library collections (see separate entry). The Cathedral and the Heritage Centre have teamed up to put many of the Roman objects on a special website (www. cathedral.southwark.anglican.org/visiting/exhibitions-and-installations/romano-southwark-online-exhibition). These objects include a section of tombstone dedicated by a woman to a man called Matrona, a fragment of a chest used to store cremated human remains and a statue of a hunter god, which is on display in the cathedral entrance. The grounds are beautiful and an ideal place to get away from the bustle of nearby Borough Market.

Directions & Accessibility: Close to London Bridge station and on the northern side of Borough Market, Southwark Cathedral can be accessed through a courtyard on its northern side, opposite the River Thames. The best location to see the Roman remains is to the left of the cathedral on entering the building. The exposed brickwork shows different periods of activity, including a section of Roman road. There is also an online exhibition of Roman remains on the cathedral website (link above). The building is historic, but almost fully accessible for those with limited mobility.

52 | Winchester Palace | Clink Street | Winchester Square
Wharf | Bathhouse | No Facilities | London Bridge
SE1 9LS | TQ 325 803 | gift.circle.coach

A little to the north-west of Southwark Cathedral, in the area crossed by Clink and Cathedral Streets, was once a bustling and busy suburb. In the medieval period, this was the site of Winchester Palace, a thirteenth-century set of buildings which were home to the bishops of Winchester. The palace burned down in 1814, although part of the Great Hall survived and can be seen as a ruin on Clink Street. Redevelopment works in the area have revealed previously unknown Roman buildings, with masonry, including painted plaster, tiles and general rubble uncovered during excavation. There was suggestion that the masonry may have been dumped into an old *hypocaust* system, although not enough of the site was excavated to confirm this.

Slightly further west, at Winchester Square, archeologists have found evidence of a substantial Roman building facing onto the Thames waterfront. The building was occupied from early in the second century, through to at least the middle of the third century, although some archaeologists speculate it was still in use at the beginning of the fourth century. The building was impressive and at its peak had some of the most ornate and best decorated walls to be found in London. Off a central courtyard was a bathhouse and additional rooms. One find discovered during the excavation of the bathhouse was a list of soldiers and the unit they belonged to, which has since led to speculation that the site had a military function.

Directions & Accessibility: There are no Roman remains to be seen at this location.

53 | The Liberty of Southwark
Mansio | Mosaic | No Facilities | London Bridge
Southwark Street | SE1 2PF | TQ 324 801 | hurry.patio.souk
www.thelibertyofsouthwark.com

Today, Southwark Street and the wider area has its fair share of pubs, restaurants and hotels, and it was no different 2,000 years ago as a Roman *mansio*, a sort of hotel for officials, was located here. Roman buildings have been known about in this area since the 1980s, so it was unsurprising that more were found in advance of the construction of the Liberty of Southwark building. One of the most notable discoveries from the *mansio* site was a substantial and very well-preserved mosaic which may have been the centrepiece of an ornate, blue plastered dining room. Dining in Roman times would have involved lying down on couches, giving the guests an opportunity to admire the ornate floor. The mosaic was designed by a craftsman who had undertaken mosaics elsewhere, with similar designs found in Trier, Germany, and probably dates to the late second or early third centuries. Beneath this was another, earlier mosaic, showing that the owners of the building were trying to keep up with the fashions.

Next to the *mansio* site was another building which also appears to have had wealthy owners given the finds recovered from the site, as well as the discovery of elaborate mosaic floors and plastered walls. Many of the finds excavated at the Liberty of Southwark site can be seen on their website, although the longer term plans are to put them on public display, either at the Museum of London or a location near to where they were excavated.

Directions & Accessibility: At the time of writing, the Liberty of Southwark building was under construction and the arrangements for seeing the mosaic and the finds from the site have not been announced.

54 | Greenwood Theatre (New Guy's House)
Boat | No Facilities | London Bridge
No. 55 Weston Street | SE1 1YR | TQ 328 799 | voice.given.audit

In 1958, during construction of the Greenwood Theatre, part of Guy's Hospital, archaeologists uncovered a previously undetected ship. The vessel itself was lying in a silted-up creek and dated to the Roman period. Only the northern part of the vessel was uncovered, with the rest being protected as a Scheduled Monument beneath the ground to this day. From the limited archaeological evidence available, the boat had a shallow draft of around a metre, was flat-bottomed and may have been as long as 16 metres and about 4.25 metres wide. Archaeologists think the vessel was a river barge, used in the shallows of the Thames and surrounding tributaries. As the vessel had a pointed end, it was not suitable for transporting cattle or wagons, and the loading of cargo would have been done at the side of the ship. This argument is supported by the discovery of a wooden quay nearby. The dating for the wreck was taken from silt samples from the area surrounding the ship, giving a date of CE 190 to 225. Rubbish was apparently dumped to the north of the vessel, in the same creek, probably cutting off access to the river, so later than the abandonment of the boat. This indicates that it may have been abandoned around the end of the second century CE.

Directions & Accessibility: There are no Roman remains visible at this site. A few surviving fragments of the boat can be seen in the Shipwreck Museum in Hastings.

Central London: East

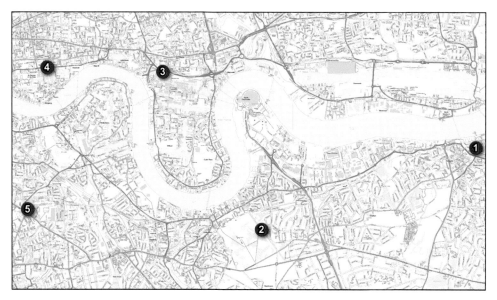

Roman sites to the east of central London.

The River Thames has played a central role in the history of Londinium, and its predecessors. Just like today, 2,000 years ago the east end of London was a hub of trade and commerce, and home to thousands of people. The Romans have left their mark on the surrounding area, with a temple and a road running through Greenwich to a high-status settlement at Shadwell.

1 | Royal Arsenal (Woolwich)
Remains | Statue | No Facilities | Woolwich
The Royal Brass Foundry, No. 1 Street, Royal Arsenal, Riverside | SE18 6GH | TQ 437 790 | exists.visa.vital

Roman statue of Deus Lunus at the Royal Arsenal, Woolwich.

In poor condition, and almost forgotten, the Roman statue of Deus Lunus (the male embodiment of the moon) stands up against part of the old Royal Brass Foundry buildings in Woolwich. It is a curious relic and was dug up by soldiers in Egypt early in the nineteenth century, before being shipped back to Britain. Presumably those soldiers were based at the Woolwich arsenal or one of the nearby barracks which is why it ended up here.

In 2018, during construction of new flats on the Royal Arsenal site, a ditch dating to the Roman period was discovered. It was 1.5 metres wide and over half a metre deep, with various finds discovered within it, leading to the suggestion that it was either a drainage or boundary ditch for some forgotten Roman settlement or fortification.

Directions & Accessibility: The statue is located on the eastern side of the Royal Brass Foundry buildings. The area is fully accessible.

2 | Greenwich Park
Remains | Temple | No Facilities | Maze Hill
SE3 7UB | TQ 392 774 | noble.riding.cities
www.royalparks.org.uk/parks/greenwich-park/things-to-see-and-do/ancient-greenwich/roman-remains

Greenwich Park seems to have had some importance to the Romans. Legend has it that Watling Street, the Roman road linking Londinium to Rochester in Kent, ran across the park. In 1433, the road was diverted to enable the area to become a deer park for Humphrey, Duke of Gloucester. The diverted Roman road appears to have formed the eastern boundary of the deer park, now Maze Hill. Eventually, the deer park gave way to a more recognisable Greenwich Park towards the end of the seventeenth century. A series of test excavations, early in the twentieth century, attempted to look for the original line of the Roman road, and it seems likely that Vanbrugh Park, to the south-east of Greenwich Park, follows the line of it. While the archaeological evidence as to whether or not the Roman road crossed over Greenwich is inconclusive, given the number of Roman finds in the area, it is more than likely that Watling Street crossed here before the Duke of Gloucester had it moved.

Assuming that the Roman road between Londinium and Rochester crossed Greenwich Park, then it would have passed close to a Roman temple. Initially uncovered around 1902 during routine maintenance in the park, three separate sections of flooring, along with building rubble and a hoard of coins were discovered. The site was further excavated in the late 1970s, and again in the late 1990s, with archaeologists concluding that there were two buildings on top of each other, with some further structures to the immediate east. The first building on the temple site was constructed from timber, around CE 100, and had a courtyard. It probably burnt down, before being completely demolished and replaced with a similar courtyard building, but which had plaster walls and a tessellated floor. The temple seems to have

Roman temple site within Greenwich Park.

finally been abandoned around the early fifth century. Other finds from this part of Greenwich Park include a road surface immediately to the south of the site, a marble tablet, animal bones, pottery and coins. The evidence strongly suggests that these buildings were a temple or religious site, particularly because of the proximity to a major road out of Londinium.

Greenwich Park is home to many historic features, all of which are worth seeking out, including Queen Caroline's bath in the south-west area of the park. These are the surviving remains of Montague House which was demolished in 1815, leaving only a bath behind. There is also an early medieval burial ground, comprising a series of thirty-one burial mounds which were almost flattened in the nineteenth century.

Directions & Accessibility: The remains of the Roman temple are located on the eastern edge of the park. The temple platform is visible as a grassed mound, with interpretation signage near where Bower Avenue and Great Cross Avenue meet. At the time of writing, the tessellated floor is not on display at the site. The park is paved and access is good, although there are uneven, grassed surfaces, particularly near the temple site.

3 | Museum of London Docklands
Museum | Café | Toilets | Westferry
No. 1 Warehouse, West India Quay | E14 4AL | TQ 372 805 | human.tent.dart
www.museumoflondon.org.uk/museum-london-docklands

Based in an old warehouse, the museum has lots of nautical- and trade-themed objects, as well as a recreation of the dark and dangerous streets of old, maritime London. There is little reference to Roman Londinium, but that does not make the museum any less interesting.

Directions & Accessibility: The museum is located a short ride on the Docklands Light Railway (DLR) from Central London or from the Underground hub of Canary Wharf. The museum is fully accessible and has regular activities for families.

4 | Shadwell
Bathhouse | No Facilities | Shadwell
Eluna Apartments, No. 4 Wapping Lane | E1W 3BE | TQ 348 806 | will.habit.cars

A little to the east of Londinium, at Shadwell, was another Roman settlement. Located alongside an early road, now known as the Highway, it seems to have developed in the middle of the third century and survived until the fifth century. Given its position, which was closer to the foreshore of the Thames back then than it is today, the settlement was focussed around a port or quay, possibly replacing those in Londinium. Previous Roman discoveries in the Shadwell area include a stone coffin recorded in St Paul's churchyard in 1858, and a number of high-status burials which were discovered nearby in the 1970s.

   Work in the twenty-first century, undertaken in advance of construction and development of new apartments, focussed on two adjacent areas at the former Tobacco Docks. These excavations uncovered third- and fourth-century timber buildings, and revealed a substantial bathhouse. Overlooking the river, the bathhouse was unusually large for such a small settlement, and it is not clear if it was a public or military building, or a private bathhouse attached to a villa. An additional building to the north of the bathhouse has been interpreted as being an accommodation block for the bathhouse workers. The bathhouse appears to have been deliberately destroyed around the beginning of the fifth century. A little to the east of the bathhouse, archaeologists uncovered the remains of a small square building which was originally interpreted as a Roman signal tower. However, more recent reassessment of the structure has indicated that it may have been a mausoleum. This seems a more likely explanation given its location just outside of the settlement, and because of the nearby high-status baths which suggest people with power and money were living here, and had the wealth to enable construction of such a building.

Directions & Accessibility: Although the remains of the bathhouse were well-preserved, standing to a height of 1.3 metres in some places, there are no visible remains on display.

5 | Old Kent Road Mural
Mural | No Facilities | South Bermondsey
Nos 600–608 Old Kent Road | SE15 1JB | TQ 344 778 | bend.foil.over

Although not a Roman site, the Old Kent Road Mural depicts Roman life in the borough of Southwark. Created in 1965 by artist Adam Kossowski, the mural is made up of thousands of ceramic pieces and depicts the history of the Old Kent Road, which was originally part of the Roman Road, Watling Street, which ran from Londinium to Rochester, Canterbury, and ending up at Dover.

There are three parts to the mural, beginning with the Romans, then moving into the early medieval period, before the third panel brings the story up to date with the 1960s. The Roman panel depicts life in Londinium, and features a temple, triumphal arch, aqueduct, an altar, Roman citizens, officials and a legionary soldier carrying a set of military standards.

Directions & Accessibility: The mural is attached to a building on the corner of the Old Kent Road and Peckham Park Road, with the Roman section facing the latter. It is fully accessible.

Central London: West

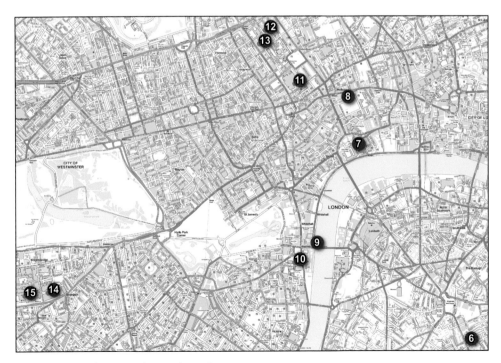

Roman sites to the west of central London.

This part of Central London is much less about physical Roman remains in the landscape, and much more about cultural exploration of the past through the museums and heritage centres which can be found here. From displays of coins and small fragments of pottery to a replica of the colossal Trajan's Column, don't forget that there are still a few physical remains to be seen if you know where to look.

6 | Southwark Heritage Centre and Walworth Library
Museum | Toilets | Elephant and Castle
Nos 145–147 Walworth Road | SE17 1RW | TQ 322 785 | piano.hiking.energy
www.heritage.southwark.gov.uk

The artefacts held by the Southwark Heritage Centre include objects from across the borough and beyond, and also incorporate the Cuming Collection. Over 25,000 objects were originally brought together by the Cuming family in the eighteenth and nineteenth centuries. The collection was on display in its own museum until 2013, when a fire damaged the building housing it, but luckily most of the objects were preserved. Part of the collection is now on display in the Heritage Centre, with many more objects displayed on their website. There are a number of Roman objects in the Cuming Collection, including those discovered within Southwark Cathedral during the 1977 excavations. These include a rare surviving example of a wooden folding stool, fragments of pottery and pieces of *hypocaust*.

Directions & Accessibility: The Heritage Centre is located on the corner of Walworth Road and Heygate Street, and is fully accessible. There are regular exhibitions of objects from the collections across the local area, as well as online.

7 | Strand Lane Roman Baths
Remains | Baths | No Facilities | Temple
No. 5 Strand Lane | WC2R 2NA | TQ 308 808 | locate.parade.tame
www.nationaltrust.org.uk/features/strand-lane-roman-baths

Hidden away in suburban London, the Strand Lane Baths, otherwise known as the Roman Bath, are actually no such thing. Research undertaken in 2012 has shown that the 'bath' was originally a cistern which supplied water to a fountain in the gardens of Old Somerset House. The fountain was constructed in 1612 and only lasted until the 1640s when it was demolished, although the cistern survived and was later opened as a public bath. The Roman connection was not made until 1838, when a reference to Roman spring baths on Strand Lane appears. The bath was refurbished in the nineteenth and early twentieth centuries, before being transferred to the care of the National Trust in the 1940s. The cistern is just over 4.5 metres long, 2 metres wide and is semicircular at one end. It is unsurprising that it was

Entrance to the Strand Lane Roman Baths.

mistaken for a Roman bath for many years given the similarities in the design of the two types of structure.

Directions & Accessibility: There are two ways of approaching the Strand Lane Baths. The first is about halfway down Surrey Street, on the right and through an archway with a sign above it, with access down Surrey Steps. However, the gate here is often closed, so the alternative route is to head down Surrey Street, turn right, then take the first right onto Strand Lane. The baths entrance is near the top of the lane, in a white building surrounded by black railings, but it is poorly signposted. The actual baths are within the basement of the building, and access is limited and opening times infrequent (and often inaccurate online). It is recommended that access is confirmed in advance of visiting. The site has steps and access may be limited for those with mobility issues.

8 | Sir John Soane Museum
Museum | Toilets | Holborn
No. 13 Lincoln's Inn Fields | WC2A 3BP | TQ 307 814 | cargo.cable.hats
www.soane.org

The Sir John Soane Museum is best described as eclectic; an odd but interesting collection of random objects. It is a diverse collection of antiquities, furniture and artworks which were collected by Sir John Soane. He died in 1837, and the collection is now displayed in his London townhouse. There are some, but not many, Roman objects in the collection. Keep your eye open for the Roman Corinthian capital (the ornate top of a column) which originally came from the Villa Adriana – the summer house of the Emperor Hadrian in Tivoli, Italy. Another piece to look out for is the large, marble lion's paw which probably came from the leg of a piece of Roman furniture.

The museum is packed full of curios and some bizarre objects picked up by Sir John Soane, and is well worth a visit if only to experience one of London's odder museums. There are regular special exhibitions and events, including a recommended highlights tour for those who have limited time.

Directions & Accessibility: The museum is located on the north side of Lincoln's Inn Fields and is easy to find. Most of the building is accessible and there are lifts, but the museum is housed within an old building and the space can be quite cramped and busy with people at peak times.

9 | Boadicea and Her Daughters Statue (Westminster Bridge)
Statue | No Facilities | Westminster
Westminster Bridge (western end) | SW1A 2JH | TQ 303 796 | strict.powers.agree

No trip to London can be complete without looking at the famous statue *Boadicea and Her Daughters* which stands in the shadow of the Houses of Parliament. The statue depicts the Queen of the Iceni tribe (whose name was actually Boudica), along with her two daughters who are riding on a chariot.

Around CE 60 to 61, Boudica led a revolt of large parts of the indigenous population against the Roman occupiers in retaliation for the sexual assault of her daughters by soldiers. As part of the revolt, Londinium was sacked and many of the buildings burned to the ground – archaeologists still find a layer of burning when excavating through the Roman layers in the city. *Boadicea And Her Daughters* was initially commissioned in 1851 from Thomas Thornycroft, who completed a model of the statue before he died in 1865. It was not until 1898 that enough money was raised to pay for the casting of the statue, but once it had been cast, there was no site agreed upon to display it, so it was not until 1902 that it was finally erected in its current location.

Directions & Accessibility: The statue is on a plinth guarding the northern side of the western end of Westminster Bridge, opposite the Queen Elizabeth Tower (which houses Big Ben) at the Houses of Parliament. Disappointingly, views of the statue are often obstructed by the souvenir stand which sits at its base.

10 | Westminster Abbey
Building | Sarcophagus | Museum | Café | Toilets | Westminster
No. 20 Deans Yard | SW1P 3PA | TQ 300 794 | laser.pencil.moral
www.westminster-abbey.org

Westminster is another part of modern London which was occupied in the Roman period, and plenty of glimpses have come to light during work at the abbey. Finds include a sarcophagus found on the north side of the abbey in 1869, and which had been reused by someone in the medieval period, a large key and a dump of rubbish.

As well as artefacts, Roman buildings have been found within the abbey. In 1878, part of a *hypocaust* was uncovered, along with a section of Roman wall, running beneath the floor of the nave. Elsewhere, Roman stones and bricks have been identified in the makeup of the walls of the abbey, particularly in the construction of the Jerusalem Chamber.

Directions & Accessibility: Located in the heart of political London, there are some Roman pieces to be seen within Westminster Abbey, with the sarcophagus on display in the Queen's Diamond Jubilee Galleries. The building is largely accessible, with further information on the website.

11 | The British Museum
Museum | Café | Toilets | Tottenham Court Road
Great Russell Street | WC1B 3DD | TQ 300 816 | awards.scared.pound
www.britishmuseum.org

The British Museum contains one of the world's greatest collections of ancient objects and artefacts from the past. However, the role and function of such institutions is increasingly coming under scrutiny, particularly surrounding objects acquired during colonial times. There is also a growing discussion on whether objects found elsewhere in Britain should be put on display in London, or closer to where they were discovered. The British Museum (or BM as it's often referred to) aims to let visitors to experience cultures from across the world, ranging from the dawn of human history to the present time, and although it does not primarily focus on the archaeology and history of Roman London, it would be remiss not to mention the museum and its collections in a volume such as this.

That said, the BM has a large collection of Roman objects from across the empire which are on display in several rooms within the museum, although most can be found in the permanent exhibition galleries: Roman Britain (Room 49), Greek and Roman life (Room 69), Roman Empire (Room 70) and Greek and Roman sculptures (Room 23). There are other related galleries such as the Etruscan World in Room 71 (the Etruscans were the predecessors of the Romans) and Britain and Europe 800 BC – AD 43 (Room 50), which covers life in Britain immediately before the Romans established themselves here.

There is not enough space in this book to cover all the Roman objects on display in the galleries, but part of the fun of visiting the BM is exploring all the nooks and crannies of this old building and discovering objects and the stories behind them. Some of the highlights include the Mildenhall Treasure (Room 49), a collection of fourth-century Roman silver which was discovered in a field in Suffolk, and an impressive collection of gold torcs (Room 50,) large, ornate necklace-style decorations worn by Iron Age people in Britain around the time that the Romans began to invade and settle. In Room 70 is the Portland Vase, an ornate blue cameo-style glass vessel which has a chequered history, including being smashed by an angry student and subsequently being rebuilt from hundreds of pieces on three occasions. It eventually made its way into the collection of the BM via the 3rd Duke of Portland (hence the name). But arguably more interesting is that the 3rd Duke lent the vase to Josiah Wedgwood who spent many years attempting to copy Roman glass-making techniques, and who replicated the style in some of his other works.

It is easy to spend most of a day or longer at the BM, given that there is so much to be seen. There are many highlights including the controversial Parthenon Sculptures (sometimes known as the Elgin Marbles), the Rosetta Stone (first used to translate Egyptian hieroglyphics), the Sutton Hoo ship burial including the iconic mask (Room 41), several Lewis Chessmen (Room 40) and so much more. With a little time, it is worth walking through the ground-floor Egyptian galleries just to see how massive and impressive some of the sculptures are. Planning is advised if there is an exhibit that you are keen to see, as some of the more popular exhibits, such as those mentioned above, can become crowded at peak times. The museum plays host to numerous exhibitions every year, although entry to these is usually by paid tickets, and occasionally there are exhibitions with a focus on Roman artefacts and sites. More information and tickets can be found on their website.

Directions & Accessibility: The BM is hard to miss, given the prominence of the building. It is fully accessible, and there is more information about this on their website. At the time of writing, visitors need to book tickets and entry slots for accessing the BM, although there is no charge. It can often be possible to book slots on the day of your visit, although at certain times of the year the museum is much busier. In the summer months, the queue for entry can be long, so be prepared to wait. Early mornings and late afternoons are often the quietest times, although there is a lot to see in the museum, so give yourself plenty of time to visit.

12 | Institute of Archaeology Collections (University College London)
Museum | Euston Square
UCL, Nos 31–34 Gordon Square | WC1H 0PY | TQ 297 823 | trip.spare.spider
www.ucl.ac.uk/culture/institute-archaeology

Few people know that the archaeological collections of the Institute of Archaeology at University College London are open to the public. The collection of some 80,000-plus objects contains a range of artefacts from different time periods, across the world, not just Roman pieces. The collection is primarily used for teaching and research and contains a significant collection of Roman and Greek pottery, as well as many plant and animal remains, and minerals. Numerous objects were recovered from work in Palestine by Sir Flinders Petrie in the late nineteenth and twentieth centuries, and the collection also contains artefacts from work in Jericho by Kathleen Kenyon. The publicly accessible collections form part of the AG Leventis Gallery of Cypriot and Eastern Mediterranean Archaeology and contain some Roman objects, but it is possible for interested members of the public to access objects not on general display by contacting the Collections Manager.

Directions & Accessibility: The collection is open weekdays and is housed in the main building of the Institute of Archaeology. Most of the collection is easily accessible, but it is an enclosed space which may limit accessibility for some.

13 | Petrie Museum of Egyptian Archaeology (University College London)
Museum | Toilets | Euston Square
UCL, Malet Place | WC1E 6BT | TQ 296 821 | thick.spots.files
www.ucl.ac.uk/culture/petrie-museum

Although people may not think of Egypt as being Roman, it was absorbed into the empire as a province (think *Antony and Cleopatra* or *Carry On Cleo*), one which was hugely important because it was the largest single supplier of grain in the Roman world, and therefore had significant strategic importance.

The Petrie Museum is a fascinating collection of some 80,000 objects covering the ancient history of Egypt and Sudan, beginning with prehistory, and also covering the pharaohs, the Ptolemaic, Roman, Coptic and Islamic periods. Originally established as a teaching resource at the end of the nineteenth century, the museum was founded using artefacts originally collected by writer Amelia Edwards, but it was the excavations in Egypt by Professor William Flinders Petrie which saw the collection massively expand. Petrie was a prolific excavator and uncovered many sites throughout Egypt, gathering up numerous artefacts which he then sold on to University College London. Given the origins of the museum, there are a large number of objects which are on display, although many of the most interesting pieces originate outside of the Roman period. One of the main highlights includes the largest collection of Roman-period mummy portraits in the world. There are many more ancient artefacts to be seen in the museum, including original clothing, stone-carved hieroglyphics, ancient art and, of course, mummy cases.

Besides the galleries, there are regular exhibition and events held in the museum, and it is even possible to view and explore the history and stories behind many of the artefacts through the museum's online collections.

Directions & Accessibility: The museum is located at the far end of a small lane which is to the north of Senate House, the main (and unmistakable) UCL building, and has a 'Petrie Museum' banner above the entrance. Although small, the museum is in an accessible building.

14 | Victoria & Albert Museum (V&A)
Museum | Café | Toilets | South Kensington
Cromwell Road | SW7 2RL | TQ 269 791 | brush.arrow.name
www.vam.ac.uk

Located in the heart of Kensington, the Victoria & Albert Museum, often just referred to as the V&A, is the marginally grander neighbour to the Natural History Museum. It is easy to spend a whole day jumping between both museums as they have quite an extensive collection of artefacts and exhibits between them, but both can get extremely busy at peak times of the day. Comprising an eclectic mix of ancient history, art, design and culture mixed in with pure Victoriana, the V&A is an experience like no other to be found in London. One minute, you can be looking at plaster casts of ancient Roman relics, and the next you can come across Elton John's Rocketman outfit! It really is an experience not to be missed.

One of the key things about the V&A is the building itself which is a complex and a marvel of Victorian engineering and architecture, and an impressive 'exhibit' in its own right. Emerging out of the Great Exhibition of 1851, the V&A was founded as a collection of the best achievements of the Victorian period, as well as pieces taken from across the British Empire and beyond. This includes numerous Roman artefacts, many of which influenced the design and architecture of the day. However, the most impressive Roman piece in the collection, and possibly in the whole museum, is the plaster cast which was taken from Trajan's Column in Rome. The original column, which sits north of the Forum in central Rome and stands around 30 metres high, was completed in CE 113 and depicts the wars between the Dacians and Romans at the beginning of the second century CE. The column is intricately carved, depicting various images from the wars, showing 155 scenes and 2,662 figures. The original column is an impressive sight, so to see an exact replica in the middle of the V&A is equally – if not more – impressive, particularly given that the column is in two parts because it is much bigger that the building housing it, and which had to be build around the column.

Other non-Roman highlights of the V&A include an extensive textile collection, with many famous and well-known designer collections, large collections of china and a lot of Victorian pieces.

Directions & Accessibility: Centrally located in Kensington, and next to the Natural History Museum, the V&A is easily discoverable in the heart of the cultural quarter. The V&A is accessible on the ground floor, but the age and design of building means that access can be more restrictive in the upper levels. More information about access, and the rest of their facilities, can be found on their website.

15 | Natural History Museum
Museum | Café | Toilets | South Kensington
Cromwell Road | SW7 5BD | TQ 266 790 | papers.quench.stack
www.nhm.ac.uk

You might think of the Natural History Museum as being full of dinosaur bones
and stuffed animals, but it also has a large collection of Roman and Iron Age
artefacts, in particular human remains collected from various excavations over the
years from across London. Not all of these remains are on display, and there are
occasional Roman focussed exhibitions. The remains give a fascinating insight to
life in Londinium, such as a collection of six individuals, uncovered in 1866 during
construction of a warehouse on the road, London Wall. The remains were first
noted in an article in *The Times*, leading to Lieutenant Colonel Augustus Lane-Fox,
who had read the piece, visiting the site that day and recording his observations.
Comprising three males and three other skeletons of undetermined sex, the remains
were passed to the Royal College of Surgeons, before eventually being donated to
the Natural History Museum. Two of the individuals suffered from severe toothache

Natural History Museum, Kensington.

and by the time of their death had already lost several teeth and were suffering from abscesses, making it painful for them to eat.

The team at the Natural History Museum undertake ongoing research into the human remains in their collection. There are frequent exhibitions and events detailing their findings and telling the stories behind the remains in their collections. Not Roman, but pieces not to be missed in the museum include their extensive collection of fossils and dinosaur remains, including a huge triceratops skull and the massive tyrannosaurus rex skeleton. In the museum entrance hall is the massive skeleton of a blue whale, and in the Earth's Treasury gallery there are real gold nuggets and gems from beneath the ground on show.

Directions & Accessibility: Located in the Kensington cultural quarter, the Natural History Museum is close to the Victoria & Albert (V&A) Museum, the Royal Albert Hall, Imperial College London, as well as Hyde Park and Harrods. The museum is easily accessed from South Kensington or Gloucester Road Underground stations. The museum is fairly accessible, although it is a Victorian building which may limit access for some. The website has more information on access.

Greater London: North

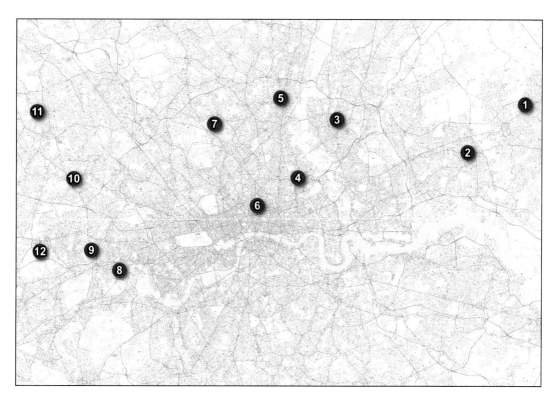

Roman sites in north Greater London.

Going beyond Central London opens up a host of new sites to be visited. In north London there are stones, bridges, museums and even pottery kilns, all with some sort of Roman connection.

1 | Romford Golf Course

Road | No Facilities | Gidea Park
Heath Drive, Gidea Park | RM2 6NB | TQ 525 902 | office.toned.kicked

Located just inside the M25, the leafy suburb of Romford hides a secret – a Roman road which runs across the greens of the local golf course. The Romford suburb of Gidea Park was constructed at the beginning of the twentieth century, although it originally belonged to Gidea Hall, and running across the parkland is a Roman road, which was identified during nearby construction work.

Directions & Accessibility: There are no visible Roman remains at this site, but the line of the road is visible across the southern half of the course and can still be followed on the ground. Romford Golf Course is private property.

2 | Valence House Museum

Museum | Café | Toilets | Chadwell Heath
Becontree Avenue, Dagenham | RM8 3HT | TQ 480 865 | abode.zealous.heap
www.valencehousecollections.co.uk

A hidden gem, Valence House has its origins as a medieval manor house, with the parts of the original moat surrounding the main buildings still surviving and in use. Focussing on objects from Barking and Dagenham, there are few Roman pieces to be seen. The library, which can be accessed by the public, has a number of good books on Roman Britain, particularly focussing on sites in Essex. There is also an exhibition space which changes regularly. The grounds and gardens are impressive, particularly in the summer months when the flowers are in full bloom.

Directions & Accessibility: Centrally located in Dagenham, Valence House is fully accessible and has lift access. The gardens may be more restrictive for some.

3 | Vestry House Museum

Museum | Café | Toilets | Walthamstow Central
Vestry Road, Walthamstow | E17 9NH | TQ 378 890 | fortunate.remove.faced
www.vestryhousemuseum.org.uk

Vestry House Museum is the local museum for the borough of Waltham Forest and has a collection of objects and stories related to the local area. The collection, of over 100,000 items, has some pieces related to Romans in the local area. There are regular exhibitions and events, including mosaic making and opportunities to meet Roman soldiers. Nearby is apparently the oldest occupied domestic dwelling in London, a fifteenth-century timber-framed hall, known as the Ancient House (No. 2 Church Lane), although it is not open to visitors.

Directions & Accessibility: Located a short walk from Walthamstow Central Underground station, the museum has limited opening hours and only the ground floor is accessible for those using wheelchairs. The museum is a Dementia Friendly Venue.

4 | Hackney Museum
Museum | Hackney Central
No. 1 Reading Lane | E8 1GQ | TQ 347 846 | reef.leads.react
www.hackney-museum.hackney.gov.uk

Located on the ground floor of a larger cultural building which includes Hackney Central Library, the museum gives a unique insight into the story of the borough of Hackney, and many of its notable residents. The museum holds various Roman objects in their collection, and have regular exhibitions and events.

Directions & Accessibility: Hackney Museum is centrally located and is fully accessible.

5 | Bruce Castle Museum
Remains | Museum | Toilets | Bruce Grove
Lordship Lane, Tottenham | N17 8NU | TQ 333 906 | farms.swift.cove
www.brucecastle.org

Set in a seventeeth-century Tudor manor house, Bruce Castle Museum has an extensive collection of artefacts representing the history of the borough of Haringey. There are several Roman objects in their collections, including artefacts associated with the nearby Roman kiln in Highgate Woods (see separate entry). The castle has regular events and exhibitions which often feature Romans. Bruce Castle Museum is set in a large and extensive parkland, and has many hidden secrets, along with a good playground and a mysterious Tudor tower.

Directions & Accessibility: Located where Bruce Grove joins Lordship Lane, Bruce Castle is unmissable. The castle is fully accessible for wheelchairs and there is a lift to all floors.

6 | Islington Museum
Museum | Farringdon
No. 245 St John Street | EC1V 4NB | TQ 316 825 | tight.extra.dads
friendsofim.com

A small museum detailing the history of Islington and its residents. The museum has a small collection of Roman artefacts and has regular events and exhibitions. At the time of writing, Islington Museum was due to undergo redevelopment, so visitors should check the museum website for further details before visiting.

Directions & Accessibility: Centrally located in Islington, the museum is close to the Roman 'heart' of London, as well as several other heritage venues, including the London Metropolitan Archives and the new Museum of London at Smithfield. The museum is fully accessible.

7 | Highgate Roman Kiln
Kiln | No Facilities | Highgate
Highgate Wood, Muswell Hill Road | N6 4HX | TQ 282 886 | badly.chase.cone
www.highgateromankiln.org.uk

Around 1962, archaeologists working in Highgate Wood found scattered fragments of Roman pottery. Following this up with an excavation four years later, they discovered an even larger amount of pottery, some of which was deliberately thrown away having been damaged during firing. They also found fragments of baked clay and other remnants which suggested that there had been large-scale pottery production at the site. Subsequent excavations in the late 1960s and early 1970s led to the discovery of a kiln which was active from around the middle of the first century CE before going out of use 100 years later. In total, ten kilns were eventually discovered, and had been used to produce kitchen and tableware. The finds from the site, including the pottery, are now held by the Museum of London (see separate entry). At the site there is a small fragment of Roman kiln to be seen, alongside some interpretation panels at the information hut in the woods, close to the Pavilion Café. There are ongoing plans to develop a visitors centre, in partnership with Bruce Castle Museum (see separate entry), with the new space opening in late 2024.

Directions & Accessibility: There are paths through the wood, but those with mobility issues may find some of these challenging.

8 | Chiswick House and Gardens
Remains | Statues | No Facilities | Chiswick
Burlington Lane | W4 2RP | TQ 209 776 | roofs.jump.soon
www.chiswickhouseandgardens.org.uk

Originally designed in the nineteenth century to show off the art collections of the 3rd Earl of Burlington, Chiswick House and Gardens was heavily inspired by the classical architecture of Rome and Italy, which Burlington experienced on his grand tours. Burlington wanted to create a Roman villa, but was also influenced by the neo-Palladian movement and Renaissance architects. This influence is obvious in several rooms within the house, as well as the overall building itself. For example, the main portico has six Corinthian columns, with the design of its door influenced by the base of Trajan's Column, and there is a bust of the Emperor Augustus, while throughout the house and gardens are many other pieces influenced by Rome. The gardens are also an attempt to recreate the landscape of Roman villas, such as the Villa Adriana (the Emperor Hadrian's summer house). It was from the Villa Adriana that three male statues, now in the gardens at Chiswick House, were taken, and identified by Daniel Defoe (the writer of *Robinson Crusoe*) as being three notable Romans – Julius Caesar, Cicero and Pompey – although it is not clear if the statues really depict them. Various other Roman-inspired statues can be seen around the gardens.

Directions & Accessibility: Located a short train ride from Central London, Chiswick House and Gardens is a great place to spend a day, with lots to do and see. Exploring the house will take up a good few hours, as will the substantial gardens. While the gardens are largely accessible, there are access limitations regarding some of the buildings, including the house, due to the historic nature of the site.

9 | Gunnersbury Park Museum
Museum | Acton Town
Gunnersbury Park House, Popes Lane | W5 4NH | TQ 186 791 | healthier.edgy.beam
www.visitgunnersbury.org/museum/

With various fragments of pottery coming from the foreshore of the Thames, and possible wooden piles in the river, along with other artefacts, it appears the area around Gunnersbury attracted attention 2,000 years ago. No significant evidence for occupation, such as a fort or civilian settlement, has yet come to light, but there was a Roman or Romano-British presence nearby.

   Gunnersbury Park Museum opened in 1929, and is housed in an early nineteenth-century mansion, the gardens of which were originally laid out in the Italian style. The museum itself is a fascinating exploration of the social and archaeological heritage and culture of Ealing and Hounslow. The displays include objects from different periods, including Roman, all from the seventeen villages which make up Ealing and Hounslow boroughs. They also include histories of some of the more well-known residents of the local area including Pocahontas and Freddie Mercury. There is also an excellent exhibition telling the story of the nearby Ealing Film Studios where many of the comedies of the 1950s were made, as well as many episodes of classic *Doctor Who*.

Directions & Accessibility: Located at the north-eastern end of a large parkland, to the west of Central London, there is plenty to do at Gunnersbury Park, including the museum along with exploring the park. Accessibility within the museum is limited due to its historic nature.

10 | Sudbury Stone
Remains | Marker Stone | No Facilities | Sudbury Town
Bridgewater Road, Greenford, Wembley | HA0 1AL | TQ 170 845 | sticks.hears.rescue

Looking like a piece of abstract art overlooking the greens of Sudbury Golf Club, the Sudbury Stone is traditionally said to mark a place where travellers would gather, and has the alternative name of the grave of the Gypsy King. However, there is another tradition that the stone was used as a boundary marker by the Roman general Julius Frontinus who was active in Britain around CE 74 to 76. The stone was originally located nearby, on Bridgewater Road, but moved to its present location during road construction in the 1950s.

Directions & Accessibility: Located to the rear of the Clubhouse at Sudbury Golf Club, the stone is set on a plinth overlooking the course. The grounds are private and the immediate landscape around the monument is paved. Permission should be sought from the clubhouse to visit the Stone.

11 | Headstone Manor and Museum
Museum | Headstone Lane
Headstone Recreation Ground, Pinner View, Harrow | HA2 6PX | TQ 141 896 | burst.
drank.dent
www.headstonemanor.org

Headstone Manor is one of the few museums in the country to still be surrounded by an original, water-filled moat. The earliest mention of a manor on the site dates back to the ninth century, although the present building was not built until 1310. There is some evidence suggestive of Roman activity in the immediate area. The manor is part of a series of historic buildings (the others include a granary, the great barn and the small barn) which tell the story of Harrow, and how the area has grown and developed through the centuries. The museum includes a collection of Roman objects, and there are regular exhibitions and events with Roman re-enactors. The museum also has artefact loan boxes for schools, covering different periods of history (including the Romans), which contain genuine ancient objects which can be handled.

Directions & Accessibility: Located slightly to the north of Harrow, accessibility at the site may be challenging for some given the historic nature of the site. The website has more information on which areas are accessible.

12 | Osterley Park Roman Bridge
Bridge | No Facilities | Hanwell
Osterley House, Jersey Road, Isleworth | TW7 4RB Bridge – UB2 4NE | TQ 144 790 |
energetic.given.bossy

Set within the grounds of the National Trust's Osterley House and Park, the Roman bridge is not actually Roman. It was built in 1780 by famed architect Robert Adam, and is constructed in a Romanesque style with an arch and Doric-style columns at either end. Until recently, the bridge was badly affected by vegetation, and although much of this has been cleared it desperately needs proper conservation and restoration work, especially as there are still tree roots growing out of it. Without such work, the bridge seems unlikely to survive for much longer. The bridge should not be mistaken for the better preserved, and less exciting bridge within the main part of Osterley Park.

Directions & Accessibility: Although technically within the grounds of Osterley House, the northern part of the park is divided by the M4. The bridge is in an uneven field and difficult to access. Permission should be sought before accessing the site.

Greater London: South

Greater London, south of the River Thames, has much to offer the curious visitor. Alleged Roman marching camps, along with tombs and villas can all be found out in

Roman sites in south Greater London.

the London suburbs. Some are easier to reach than others, and some have more to see than the rest, with one highlight being Crofton Roman villa at Orpington, a site not to be missed and within easy reach of the city.

13 | Twickenham Museum

Museum | Toilets | Twickenham
No. 25 The Embankment, Twickenham | TW1 3DU | TQ 164 732 | backup.clap.save
www.twickenham-museum.org.uk

Set in an eighteenth-century listed building, the museum covers the history of the borough of Richmond. There are some delightful curios in the museum, and although there is not a great deal connected to the Romans, there was early activity in the area, including a large stash of pottery which was discovered in nearby Lower Teddington Road in the 1990s. There are several other historic sites nearby which are worth exploring, including Marble Hill, Ham House and Garden, Sandycombe Lodge (which one belonged to the artist J. M. W. Turner) and Hampton Court Palace. The delightfully named Eel Pie Island, an artists' colony only a two-minute walk from the museum, is worth exploring.

Directions & Accessibility: Twickenham Museum is based towards the riverfront in Twickenham. It is located within a historic building, which may restrict access for some. The museum has limited opening times, with further details on their website.

14 | Mount Clare

Remains | Columns | No Facilities | Barnes
Nos 10–72 Minstead Gardens | SW15 4EE | TQ 216 740 | sleepy.desk.smiled

A Grade I listed building in Roehampton, Mount Clare was initially constructed in the latter part of the eighteenth century by Sir Robert Taylor, with Roman influences in the Romanesque design of the building, along with a classically influenced temple within the grounds. However, the temple is somewhat neglected and in danger of collapse, and fundraising is currently going on to save it and make it more accessible. The temple contains a 1760s painted ceiling, laurel wreaths, tripod burners and other symbols of classical life. There is also a relief of one panel from the Parthenon frieze (sometimes known as the Elgin Marbles and now held in the British Museum). The remains of another temple in the grounds are currently in storage and include original Roman sections.

Directions & Accessibility: Fundraising to restore the temple is currently ongoing, with access to the site, which is owned by the University of Roehampton, limited at the time of writing.

15 | Caesar's Camp (Wimbledon Common)
Hillfort | No Facilities | Raynes Park
Camp Road | SW19 4TE | TQ 223 710 | hope.newly.ridge

Once upon a time, Caesar's Camp on Wimbledon Common was quite a distinct feature in the landscape and traditionally the site of a Roman camp occupied by Julius Caesar during his initial invasion of Britain. However, the camp is not a camp and is actually an indigenous hillfort. It was surrounded by a bank and ditch, creating a secure inner enclosure, within which there would have been roundhouses where people lived. Covering an area of 0.6 hectares, it was constructed around the third century BCE, long before the Romans arrived in Britain. The connection to Julius Caesar only appears in the nineteenth century, around the time the ramparts were partially damaged by an owner who wanted to build a house on top of it. In the 1930s, when a trench was being dug to install a water pipe, evidence of timber posts which were used to support the ramparts was uncovered. Sadly, in recent decades, the site has become lost under vegetation, a golf course and nearby housing, making the ditches difficult to locate. Several sites across southern England have been given the name Caesar's Camp, and this one is not to be confused with the fort (long since disappeared) which was originally in the grounds of Holwood House in Keston.

To the north-west of Caesar's Camp, archaeologists noted a small, rectangular enclosure (TQ 2245 7173) which showed up in aerial photographs. When they investigated on the ground, they discovered a bank and ditch which ran for 60 metres and was 6.5 metres wide, with rounded corners at each end. It is unknown what the feature is, but it could be a Roman camp. There is another suggestion that it could belong to a volunteer encampment established on the common at the end of the eighteenth century.

Directions & Accessibility: Caesar's Camp is located to the north-west of the Royal Wimbledon Golf Club and Cedar Park Gardens. A path runs through the camp, although access in the area is restricted because of private property. Caesar's Camp is clearly marked on the Ordnance Survey map, although features on the ground are difficult to make out due to undergrowth. Accessibility is limited due to the uneven nature of the ground.

16 | Morden Park Mound
Barrow | No Facilities | Morden South
SM4 4BX | TQ 245 674 | burn.lands.bill

Almost in the centre of Morden Park is a raised platform which is covered in trees. The mound is around 36 metres in diameter, and surrounded by a more recent bank and ditch arrangement. This mound is believed to be a burial mound or barrow, although it is debated whether or not it dates to the Bronze Age. Its proximity to Stane Street, the Roman road running between Londinium and Chichester, has led some to suggest that it was constructed in the Roman period. However, an early nineteenth-century map shows a pagoda on the mound, and there is some suggestion that the mound may have been built to support this. Without excavation, it is difficult to conclude what the mound is, or even how old it is.

Directions & Accessibility: The barrow is recognisable as a circular area of trees, a little to the south-west of the outdoor fitness area in the centre of the park. A small track runs across the mound. It is unpaved and may limit access for some.

17 | Clapham Common
Remains | Altar | No Facilities | Clapham Common
Omnibus Theatre, No. 1 Clapham Common North Side | SW4 0LH | TQ 291 754 | food.grand.hands

In 1966, an excavation took place at No. 31 Clapham Common South Side, in advance of construction of a garage and was prompted by the discovery of a Roman lamp in the garden of a house two doors up. During the excavation, the archaeologists found some pottery which suggested pre-Roman activity in the area, but what is more interesting is that they found evidence for three phases of Roman occupation, during the late first century or early to mid-second century. This included a series of timber buildings, along with some ditches, which the excavators thought could be associated with the Roman army. By the second century, the site may have evolved into a villa or a *mansio*. However, the area is already well developed, and the excavators thought it unlikely that more evidence would come to light, and which would help to date the site and identify the function of the buildings.

   Interestingly, there is a suggestion from 1724 that there may have been a Roman road (now lost) crossing the common at some point, and which gives some support to the idea that a *mansio* exists nearby. Early in the twentieth century, during building works near Clapham Common South Side, a Roman grave marker was uncovered with an inscription which stated it was erected by Vitus Licinius Ascanius, and that he had it carved while still alive, possibly in the first century CE. The stone now stands in the grounds of the Omnibus Theatre at No. 1 Clapham Common North Side.

Directions & Accessibility: If facing the theatre building, the altar stone is in the front left corner, against the railings. Often it is partly covered by shrubbery, and the inscription has faded. The site is up a few steps, but in the grounds of the theatre.

18 | Beddington Park
Villa | No Facilities | Ampere Way
CR0 4UE | TQ 297 656 | tamed.sleep.merit

The southern suburb of Beddington is home to one of several Roman villas which are all located within the M25. Discovered in the eighteenth century and excavated in the nineteenth and throughout the twentieth centuries, the Beddington Park villa site was occupied from the earliest times. There is evidence for a prehistoric enclosed settlement on the site in the Bronze Age, and continuing through to the Iron Age when a farmstead was established. In the Roman period, a small villa, essentially a rural estate, was built at Beddington Park, although part of this was destroyed in the early twentieth century. The villa was occupied from the first century through to the fourth century, with a bathhouse added to the site in the middle of the latter period. The site was eventually abandoned around CE 400.

Directions & Accessibility: Although remains of parts of the villa survive, the site is privately owned, overgrown, and inaccessible to the public.

19 | Museum of Croydon
Museum | Café | Toilets | George Street
Croydon Clocktower, Katharine Street, Croydon | CR9 1ET | TQ 324 653 | stores.cheek.improving
www.museumofcroydon.com

This small museum and art gallery is located in one of the most impressive buildings in the area, the Croydon Clocktower, and is worth visiting for this alone. It has a small Roman and early medieval collection on the ground floor. As well as a museum, the building also houses the David Lean cinema, and a Research Room where the local archives can be accessed.

Directions & Accessibility: The Croydon Clocktower is a difficult to miss building, and is located in central Croydon. The building is fully accessible.

20 | Keston Roman Villa & Tombs
Remains | Villa | Tombs | No Facilities | Hayes
Leaves Green, Keston | BR2 6AG | TQ 414 632 | crisis.grass.panels

Keston was a site of significant activity, both in the Roman period and beyond. Located in one of the more rural parts of Bromley, the remains of several Roman burial structures are visible today. The remains were discovered at Keston in the eighteenth century, but it was not until the 1820s that the first excavations took place. This led to the uncovering of a round mausoleum, with further work later in the century revealing the villa. It was not until the second half of the twentieth century that more of the villa site was excavated, with the results indicating that the immediate area was initially occupied several thousand years before the Romans. Activity at the site seems to have been sporadic until around 50 BCE when a small farmstead may have been constructed on the site. After a hundred years or so, the site had developed and a small cemetery was created. In the latter part of the first century CE, a series of wooden buildings was established, probably forming the first farm complex or villa estate, although these did not last long.

By the second century, most of the villa buildings had been replaced in stone, with evidence for some of these having painted rooms, showing that the owners had wealth and status. However, it did not last, and at some point during the third century, buildings fell out of use, and less than 100 years later the villa was abandoned. But this is not the end of the story at Keston, as in the middle of the fifth century, the site was reoccupied, and an early medieval village was established, lasting for 100 years. The cemetery seems to have been in use throughout the second and third centuries and into the fourth century CE, and goes beyond the area just outside the villa buildings.

Directions & Accessibility: The remains of the round mausoleum and some additional tomb foundations can be seen, although the latter are not as well preserved. The tombs are located within an area of private housing, although the Kent Archaeological Society occasionally hosts open days at the site. The site is mainly grass, with some lumps and bumps, which may be hazardous for some.

21 | Crofton Roman Villa

Remains | Villa | Museum | Toilets | Charge | Orpington
Crofton Road, Orpington | BR6 8AF | TQ 454 658 | narrow.give.pest
www.karu.org.uk/crofton_roman_villa.html

The earliest activity at Crofton was an Iron Age hut which dates to around 100 BCE, but by the middle of the first century CE there is evidence of a small farm or farmstead having been established here. This was later replaced in the second century by the buildings which form the remains visible today, and activity at the site lasted until some point in the fifth century.

Crofton Roman Villa was part of an extensive estate, comprising domestic and farm buildings, surrounded by fields which were used for agricultural production. The main building is the villa, around 40 metres long and 15 metres wide, although archaeologists found it had been redeveloped and expanded several times throughout its lifetime and at one point may have had more than twenty rooms. The villa comprised a main corridor on the west side, with five rooms off this and another corridor and rooms on the east side, which were added at a later date. At some point, a section of the villa on the north side of the site may have been destroyed, while other rooms were abandoned, perhaps due to a downturn in the fortunes of the site. The entire site was abandoned around CE 400, with the remaining buildings falling into disrepair and collapsing as the site eventually disappeared beneath the ground.

The villa was first discovered in the nineteenth century, but it was not until the twentieth century that the site was periodically excavated and the remains eventually put on display. The main corridor of the villa and five rooms off this can be seen today, along with the remains of the *hypocaust*, with the stoke holes being visible in the remaining rooms. Run by Kent Archaeological Rescue Unit, the site has regular events, along with object handling and a gift shop.

Directions & Accessibility: The site is to the west of Orpington station and has seasonal opening hours. Accessibility is partially limited around the historic remains.

22 | Fordcroft Bathhouse
Remains | Bathhouse | No Facilities | St Mary Cray
Bellefield Road, Orpington | BR5 2DH | TQ 467 675 | strong.signal.snacks
www.odas.org.uk/roman-bath-house

The remains here are all that survive of a bathhouse which probably belonged to a villa estate or Roman settlement nearby. The remains of three rooms are visible, with the walls surviving to a height of half a metre. In total, the length of the remains are 45 metres long and about 3.5 metres wide, while the room on the east side has an apse or a semi-circular recess, a feature commonly found in bathhouses. The building had a *hypocaust* to heat the rooms, and further work by archaeologists has indicated that there are more rooms surviving underground, including a paved courtyard and other buildings. Evidence of slag from the site indicates that in the Roman period, industrial workings were taking place here, although it is not clear if this was contemporaneous with the use of the site as a bathhouse.

The site was discovered in the 1940s during road works, and this led to excavation which initially uncovered part of the site, although there have been further excavations with finds including pottery, *hypocaust,* roof tiles and fragments of mosaic.

Directions & Accessibility: Covering an area between Poverest Road and Fordcroft Road, the remains are located in an open-ended building in a small, grassed enclosure which is accessible through a gate on Bellefield Road. The bathhouse is only open on certain days, with tours organised by the Orpington and District Archaeological Society. There is no formal path at the site which may limit accessibility for some.

Beyond London

From palaces to native settlements, from cities of the empire to amphitheatres and fortresses, there are hundreds of Roman sites beyond London, many within easy reach of the capital. Below are just a few locations which are worth visiting if you want to see more remains of the Roman Empire.

Bath
www.romanbaths.co.uk

Possibly one of the best-known Roman towns in Britain, Bath was the site of thermal springs which the Romans developed into a substantial bathing complex and religious shrine. Known as Aquae Sulis, the thermal waters still pour into large pools which the Romans bathed in. The spring itself is the location of a shrine to the goddess Minerva. The site was further developed in the Georgian period as people flocked to the town to 'take the waters', which can still be drunk today, although it is an acquired taste.

Canterbury
www.canterburymuseums.co.uk/canterbury-roman-museum

Durovemum Cantiacorum began life as an indigenous settlement established at a crossing point over the River Stour, and where roads between several Roman settlements (Dover, Richborough, Reculver and Lympne) converged. Its strategic position on the road network led to its growth as a Roman town, with a temple, basilica forum, baths and theatre being established in the latter half of the first century CE. By the third century, the town had been surrounded by walls, and occupation continued until after the official departure of the Romans in 410, probably because of close links with Gaul. There are several Roman sites to be seen in the area, including the *hypocaust* of the Butchery Lane townhouse, while many finds from the town (including a well-preserved mosaic) are on display in Canterbury Roman Museum.

Chichester
The West Sussex town of Chichester, known as Noviomagus Reginorum to the Romans, began life as a settlement of a local tribe, the Atrebates. Once the Romans arrived, the settlement grew into a Roman town with the construction of various civic buildings, including an amphitheatre, bathhouses, temples, along with aqueducts and industrial workings. In the second century, a wall was constructed around the town, and just like the London Wall, this was strengthened in the medieval period, and further refined in Victorian times. The Roman settlement seems to have been abandoned towards the end of the fourth century, but was again occupied by the eighth century. Visible Roman remains include some sections of the town walls, a mosaic which can be seen beneath the cathedral and a bastion. While the Novium Museum contains many Roman finds from across Chichester, Fishbourne Roman Palace and Gardens is close to the town and also worth visiting (see below).

Colchester
Frequently referred to as the first city of Roman Britain, Colchester (Camulodunum) was the first settlement which was established by the Romans when they invaded in 43 BCE. Within easy reach of London, Colchester has a wealth of Roman remains which have survived, included large sections of the original city walls (later reused in the medieval period), along with two surviving gates (the Balkerne Gate and Duncan's Gate). Colchester Castle and Museum, built on top of the Temple of Claudius, also has a large collection of Roman artefacts on display. Colchester also has the only known Roman Circus in Britain. This was a 450-metre-long circuit

which charioteers raced around, while 8,000 Roman citizens watched on, with part of the site still visible today.

Dover

For almost 2,000 years, Dover (Dubris) has been one of the main ports for entry into Britain. In Roman times it was not much different as Dover had a large harbour flanked by two lighthouses and may even have been the base of the Classis Britannica, the Roman fleet in Britain. The importance of the area is reflected in the discovery of over sixty Roman buildings in this part of Kent. Roman sites which can be visited include Dover Castle, where the only surviving Roman lighthouse in Britain can be seen. One particular dwelling worth visiting and described as the finest Roman house in Britain, is the Painted House. It was built around CE 200 and was most likely a *mansio* or hotel for officials of the empire. The house is the only place in Britain where painted walls or murals dating back to Roman times can be seen in their original location. Dover Museum, which has Roman objects on display, is also worth exploring.

Exeter

Slightly further afield from London, Exeter (Isca) is one of the main military sites of early Roman Britain, with a legionary fortress established here around the middle of the first century CE. Sections of the Roman wall, which surrounded the city, can be seen in various locations, while the Royal Albert Memorial Museum has an assortment of finds from across Exeter.

Fishbourne Roman Palace and Gardens

The largest known Roman residence north of the Alps, Fishbourne Roman Palace and Gardens is located in West Sussex, close to the Roman town of Chichester and not too distant from London. Initially constructed around CE 75, the palace began life as military granary before being redeveloped into a residence. With four wings surrounding a large, open courtyard, baths, along with ornate mosaic floors and painted scenes covering the walls, indicate this was a residence of some importance. Most of the site has been excavated, and the remains preserved for visitors to see. There is also a museum housing the finds recovered from the site.

Hadrian's Wall

Emperor Hadrian came to the Roman province of Britannia 1,900 years ago and commanded that a wall was to be built to keep the barbarians out of the empire. The wall stretches for some 135 kilometres (84 miles) across the north of England, from Newcastle upon Tyne in the east, to Carlisle in the west. It was not just a wall, but a system of forts, milecastles and turrets all interconnected and designed to stop enemy attackers and control the movement of the indigenous population. Today, large sections of the wall survive, alongside the remains of the fortifications and even the most northerly Roman town in the world at Corbridge. The forts (and museums) at Vindolanda, Housesteads, Chesters and Birdoswald offer some unique insights into life on the edge of the Roman world for both soldiers and civilians. There are also two major museums to see at opposite ends of the wall: Tullie House Museum in Carlisle and the Great North Museum at Newcastle. Both museums have extensive Roman collections. There are also excavations to be seen in the summer months at Vindolanda, Birdoswald and Carvoran, while there is ongoing work at the fort bath in Carlisle. Individual websites for these sites will contain up-to-date information.

Lincoln

www.visitlincoln.com/trails/roman-heritage-trail-of-lincoln

Lincoln (Lindum Colonia), like Canterbury and York, was at one point, the regional headquarters for the Roman army. This led to the rapid establishment of a settlement outside the walls of the legionary fortress, and one which continued to grow after the Romans had gone, becoming a major religious centre in the medieval period. The Lincoln skyline is dominated by the cathedral and castle, as well as the city walls, all of which were influenced by the remains of the Roman fortress and adjacent settlement. Highlights include the castle and cathedral, as well as the East Gate and the Newport Arch (a Roman gate which still has traffic passing through it), while it is still possible to see wheel ruts in a section of Roman road which runs beneath St Mary's Guildhall. The Visit Lincoln website has an excellent Roman tour of the city which visitors can use to navigate their way around the ancient sites.

Saxon Shore Forts

As Roman Britain declined, towards the late third century, the territory faced a series of challenges, including physical attacks from Continental Europe, but also civil war and a succession of emperors. This was not helped by a reduction in the number of soldiers stationed in Britain at the time. These threats led to the construction of a series of Roman forts on the south-eastern coast of Britain, and which became known as the Saxon Shore Forts. There were nine forts: Brancaster and Burgh Castle in Norfolk, Bradwell-on-Sea in Essex, Reculver, Richborough, Dover Castle and Lympne in Kent, Pevensey Castle in East Sussex, and Portchester Castle in Hampshire. Many of these sites still exist today and can be visited, although most have been developed and rebuilt since the Roman period. The museum at Richborough has a dedicated display on the Saxon Shore Forts and the Roman finds at that site.

Scotland

There are over 300 Roman sites across Scotland, and there is even a Roman wall, the Antonine Wall, running almost between Edinburgh and Glasgow for almost 58 kilometres, with many of the sites along it being some of the best-preserved sites in Scotland. There are extensive Roman collections in the Hunterian Museum (Glasgow) and the National Museum of Scotland (Edinburgh), as well as at the Trimontium

Museum at Melrose in the Scottish Borders, which is also Scotland's only museum wholly dedicated to the Romans.

Silchester

Calleva Atrebatum, otherwise known as Silchester, is an abandoned Roman town in Berkshire. Starting life as a native settlement around the first century BCE, Silchester rapidly grew to become a major Roman town with construction of walls, a basilica forum, street grids and an amphitheatre. However, unlike most similar settlements which continued to develop and grow and are still major towns and cities today, Silchester seems to have been completely abandoned sometime around the fifth or sixth century. There are several reasons why this might have been, but it seems most likely that it was overtaken as a regional capital city by the development of nearby Winchester in the early medieval period. Today, visitors can still walk the city walls which survive to an impressive height, visit the remains of the amphitheatre or observe the excavations which take place at the site every year.

St Albans

www.stalbansmuseums.org.uk

One of the best-preserved Roman sites in Britain, St Albans, then known as Verulamium, was the third largest city in Britannia, and had an extensive collection of Roman buildings. St Albans Museum has a major collection of artefacts, including some of the finest mosaics in the Roman world. It is possible to follow the line of the original Roman city wall which was 5 metres high and almost 4 kilometres long. Verulamium Park contains many of the remains of Roman buildings, including a superbly preserved mosaic, sections of *hypocaust* and the city walls. There is also the only surviving remains of a Roman theatre in Britain.

Welwyn Roman Baths

www.millgreenmuseum.co.uk

The Roman baths, located a little to the north of Welwyn Garden City and within easy reach of London, were part of a wider villa complex which has since been destroyed by construction of the A1(M). Luckily, most of the baths were preserved, although a large section lies 9 metres beneath the motorway. Discovered and excavated in 1960, the baths and villa have been dated to the third century, with sections of the former now preserved within a concrete chamber underneath the motorway and accessible through a tunnel.

York

Almost 2,000 years ago, a Roman legionary fortress was established at York, becoming the regional headquarters of the military, controlling the north of England and Scotland. More or less as soon as the fortress was established, a settlement grew up around it, developing into a major town, much in the same way as Londinium established itself. Eboracum, as it was known to the Romans, evolved in the Jorvik of the Vikings and then the York of today. Surrounded by some of the most complete medieval city walls (with Roman foundations) in Britain, there are dozens of Roman sites to be seen, and given that the city is only a few hours from London by train, it is a must see for anyone interested in Roman remains. From bits of the legionary fortress *principia* (headquarters building) beneath the main towers of the Minster (and where the Emperor Septimius Severus is said to have died), to the remains of a bathhouse in the cellars of a pub, there is plenty to do and see. The Yorkshire Museum has a large collection of Roman objects, and is set within a park with the remains of a medieval monastery to be seen, as well as numerous Roman stone coffins. Currently, a large section of the fortress is being excavated to create a Jorvik-style Roman experience, provisionally entitled Eboracum. Besides the Roman remains, there is the Jorvik Viking Centre, where there are tours of York in Norse times, and there are plenty of medieval churches and halls to be seen. The Castle Museum is also a great experience, with Civil War armour and recreated Victorian streets to be toured.

Part 5: Finding Out More

There are many ways to find out more about Roman archaeology in London and beyond, including through archaeology and history groups and societies. Many of these are listed below and focus on London and the surrounding area, but there are also national organisations such as the Council for British Archaeology and the Society of Antiquaries of London. Many of the societies regularly produce monographs and journals which contain details of Roman finds and excavations which have taken place across the city and beyond. Back issues of many archaeological journals, monographs and unpublished volumes (known as grey literature) can be found through the Archaeological Data Service or through individual society websites.

Many of the societies and groups, along with the museums and institutions detailed earlier in this book, organise regular lectures and events, many of which are open to non-members and can be viewed online. Many also sponsor, support or undertake their own excavations, which volunteers can take part in or visit as part of organised tours, so it is always worth checking out their websites for the latest information. Larger excavations across the capital are undertaken by professional archaeological units, such as MOLA (Museum of London Archaeology), but sadly are often inaccessible to the public, as they are part of larger construction projects. However, there are occasional tours and open days for some of these projects, and it is also worth checking local media and individual unit websites.

Societies and Groups

Association for Roman Archaeology – associationromanarchaeology.org
Bexley Archaeological Group – bag.org.uk
Brentford and Chiswick Local History Society – brentfordandchiswicklhs.org.uk
British Archaeological Association – thebaa.org
Camden History Society – camdenhistorysociety.org
Canterbury Archaeological Trust – canterburytrust.co.uk
Carshalton and District History and Archaeology Society – cadhas.org.uk
City of London Archaeological Trust – colat.org.uk
City of London Archaeology Society – colas.org.uk
Council for British Archaeology – archaeologyuk.org

Council of British Archaeology in London – archaeologyinlondon.com
EMAS Archaeological Society – emasarchaeology.org
Enfield Archaeological Society – enfarchsoc.org
English Heritage – english-heritage.org.uk
Essex Society for Archaeology and History – esah1852.org.uk
Greenwich Historical Society – ghsoc.co.uk
Hendon and District Archaeological Society – hadas.org.uk
Institute of Historical Research – history.ac.uk
Islington Archaeology and History Society – islingtonhistory.org.uk
Kent Archaeological Society – kentarchaeology.org.uk
London and Middlesex Archaeological Society – lamas.org.uk
Merton Historical Society – mertonhistoricalsociety.org.uk
National Trust – nationaltrust.org.uk
Orpington and District Archaeological Society – odas.org.uk
Richmond Archaeological Society – richmondarchaeology.org.uk
Roman Roads Association – romanroads.org
Roman Society – romansociety.org
Royal Archaeological Institute – royalarchinst.org
Society of Antiquaries of London – sal.org.uk
Southwark and Lambeth Archaeological Society
Surrey Archaeological Society – surreyarchaeology.org.uk
Sussex Archaeological Trust – sussexpast.co.uk
Wandsworth Historical Society – wandsworthhistory.org.uk
Welwyn Archaeological Society – welwynarchaeologicalsociety.wordpress.com
West Essex Archaeological Group – weag.org.uk

Websites

Archaeological Data Service – archaeologydataservice.ac.uk
Heritage Gateway – heritagegateway.org.uk
Historic England – historicengland.org.uk
Portable Antiquities Scheme – finds.org.uk
Thames Discovery Programme – thamesdiscovery.org
Thames Estuary Mudlarking Society – mudlarkers.co.uk

Magazines

British Archaeology Magazine – www.archaeologyuk.org/what-we-do/british-archaeology-magazine.html

Current Archaeology Magazine – archaeology.co.uk

London Archaeologist – www.londonarchaeologist.org.uk

Further Reading

There have been many books written about Roman London, and there is not enough space to detail them all here. The books listed here are a sample of some of the more notable volumes covering the archaeology and history of Roman London, many of which have been consulted during the writing of this book. Many antiquarian volumes which mention Roman London are no longer in print, but can be found online through www.archive.org or can be consulted at the British Library.

Key Sources

Clarke, J., Cotton, Jonathan, Hall, Jenny, Sherris, Roz, Swain, H. (eds), *Londinium and Beyond: Essays on Roman London and Its Hinterland for Harvey Sheldon* (Council for British Archaeology, 2008)

Davies, B., Richardson, B., Tomber, R., Ramirez, R., *The Archaeology of Roman London Volume 5* (Council for British Archaeology, 1994)

Hingley, R., Unwin, C., *Boudica: Iron Age Warrior Queen* (Hambledon Continuum, 2006)

Hingley, R., *Londinium: A Biography: Roman London from its Origins to the Fifth Century* (Bloomsbury Academic, 2018)

Maiklem, L., *Mudlarking: Lost and Found on the River Thames* (Bloomsbury Circus, 2019)

Marsden, P., *Ships of the Port of London: First to Eleventh Centuries* AD (English Heritage, 1994)

Martin, C., Marsden, P., 'Ships of the Port of London: First to Eleventh Centuries AD', *Britannia*, 28 (1997), pp. 505–506

Merrifield, R., *Handbook to Roman London* (Guildhall Museum, 1973)

Merrifield, R., *London: City of the Romans* (Batsford, 1983)

Merrifield, R., *The Roman City of London* (E. Benn, 1965)

Milne, G., *Roman London* (English Heritage, 1995)

Perring, D., *London in the Roman World* (OUP, 2022)

Perring, D., Roskams, S., *The Archaeology of Roman London, Volume 2: The Early Development of Roman London West of the Walbrook* (Museum of London and the Council for British Archaeology, 1991)

Webb, S., *Life in Roman London* (The History Press, 2012)

Maps

The maps within this book contain site data extracted from various sources detailed within the text, including Historic England Research Records, the Greater London Historic Environment Record and Ordnance Survey OpenData © Crown Copyright (2023) – OS VectorMap District. http://os.uk/opendata/ licence.

Individual Site Sources

The sources detailed here is an extensive, but not exhaustive list of the main bibliographic records consulted in compiling this book. Other sources which have been consulted are contained in the general reading list. The sources are formatted as follows: Source Abbreviation – volume – (publication year) – pages.

Source Abbreviations

The following abbreviations are used for the sources consulted for the individual site entries.

AC	*Archaeologia Cantiana – Journal of the Kent Archaeological Society*
BRIT	*Britannia Journal*
HEL	Historic England Listing number (www.historicengland.org.uk/listing/the-list)
HEMN	Historic England Monument Number (www.heritagegateway.org.uk)
JBAA	*Journal of the British Archaeological Association*
JRS	*Journal of the Society for the Promotion of Roman Studies*
LA	*London Archaeologist Journal*
TLMAS	*Transactions of the London and Middlesex Archaeological Society* – lamas.org.uk

Aldermanbury: HEL 1002053; HEMN 77282; JRS 1911 (1) 141–172; JRS 1950 (40) 92–118; JRS 1958 (48) 142–144; JRS 1966 (56) 210–211; JRS 1967 (57) 190–192.

Aldersgate: HEL 1018882; HEMN 405334; HEMN 405333.

Aldgate: HEL 1002048; HEMN 405292.

All Hallows by the Tower Church: HEL 1064671.
www.ahbtt.org.uk

Amen Court: HEL 1002068.

America Square: BRIT 19 (1988) 461–462; BRIT 22 (1991) 265; HEL 1432676.

Bank of America Financial Centre: HEL 1003773.
Lyon, J., *Within these walls: Roman and medieval defences north of Newgate at the Merrill Lynch Financial Centre, City of London* (Museum of London Archaeology Service, 2007).
ianvisits.co.uk/articles/museums-by-appointment-the-london-roman-wall-and-bastion-27026

Bank of England Museum: HEL 1079134.
www.bankofengland.co.uk/museum/online-collections/blog/archaeology-at-the-bank-of-england

Barber-Surgeons' Hall: HEL 1018888.
www.barber-surgeonshall.com

Barbican Estate: HEL 1001668.

Barnet Museum: www.barnetmuseum.co.uk

Bastion House (former Museum of London): HEL 1018889.

Beddington Park: HEL 1001990.

Billingsgate | Coal Exchange: HEL 1001993; BRIT 7 (1976) 350; BRIT 14 (1983) 311; BRIT 21 (1990) 99–183; LA 7 (1996) 415–423.
www.cityoflondon.gov.uk/things-to-do/attractions-museums-entertainment/billingsgate-bathhouse

Blackfriars: Brit 28 (1997) 505–506; HEMN 405065; JRS 54 (1964) 168.
www.collection.sciencemuseumgroup.org.uk/objects/co41182/model-of-roman-ships-hull-planking-blackfriars-thames-london-model

Boadicea and Her Daughters Statue (Westminster Bridge): HEL 1237737.
www://bit.ly/3HhDnTf

Borough High Street: HEL 1422618; HEMN 966418; HEMN 1145912.
The Southwark and Lambeth Archaeological Excavation Committee, *Southwark Excavations 1972–1974* (London and Middlesex Archaeological Society and Surrey Archaeological Society Joint Publications, 1978).

British Museum: www.britishmuseum.org

Bruce Castle Museum: www.brucecastle.org

Caesar's Camp (Wimbledon Common): HEL 1002014; HEMN 401356.

Camomile Street: HEL 1005547; HEMN 405201; HEMN 405303.

Chiswick House and Gardens: HEL 1079568.
Ayres, P., *Classical Culture and the Idea of Rome in Eighteenth Century England* (Cambridge University Press, 1997).
Hewlings, R., *Chiswick House and Gardens* (English Heritage, 1989).
www.english-heritage.org.uk/visit/places/chiswick-house/history

Clapham Common: HEL 1080492; HEMN 401183; HEMN 140102; HEMN 77332; TLMAS 22 (1968) 27–32.

Cooper's Row: HEL 1002062; HEMN 405279.

Cripplegate: HEL 1018887.

Cripplegate Roman Fort: BRIT 44 (2013) 426–427; HEL 139653; HEL 405329; HEL 405322; LA 2018 (15) 137–140.
Shepherd, J., 'The discovery of the Roman fort at Cripplegate, City of London: excavations by W F Grimes 1947–68' (Museum of London Archaeology, 2012).

Crofton Roman Villa: HEL 1001992; LA 12 (2010) 244–248.
Philip, B., *A Roman Site, Station Approach, Orpington* (Kent Archaeological Rescue Unit).
Philip, B., *The Roman Villa Site at Orpington, Kent* (Kent Archaeological Rescue Unit, 1996).
www.karu.org.uk/crofton_roman_villa.html

Crossrail: www.archaeology.crossrail.co.uk/exhibits
www.mola.org.uk/blog/mystery-crossrail-skulls

www.museumoflondon.org.uk/discover/tunnel-developmental-archaeology-crossrail-docklands

Crutched Friars (Emperor House): HEL 1002069; TLMAS 31 (1980) 68–76.

Dyers' Hall: HEL 1002057; LA 16 (2021).

Fishmongers' Hall: HEL 1002058.

Fordcroft Orpington: HEL 1001973.
Philip, B., Keller, P., *The Roman Site at Fordcroft, Orpington* (Kent Archaeological Rescue Unit).
www.odassodas.org.uk/roman-bath-house

Goldsmiths' Hall: HEL 1002027.

Goring Street: HEL 1002049; HEMN 405301; HEMN 405300; HEMN 966526.

Governor's Palace: CA 8 (1968) 215–219; HEL 1001997; HEMN 405249; LA 2018 (15) 137–140; TLMAS 26 (1975) 1–102; TLMAS 29 (1978) 99–103.

Greenwich Park: HEL 1021439; HEMN 404335; HEMN 662281; HEMN 761479; HEMN 610566; HEMN 404330; HEMN 662297; LA 3 (1979) 311–317; LA 10 (2002) 46–53, 76–81; TLMAS 34 (1983) 61–65.
www.royalparks.org.uk/parks/greenwich-park/things-to-see-and-do/ancient-greenwich/roman-remains

Greenwood Theatre (New Guy's House): HEL 1001979.

Guildhall and Guildhall Yard: Brit 28 (1997) 51–85; HEL 1013411; LA 6 (1990) 232–241; LA 7 (1994) 258–262.
Bateman, N., *Roman London's Amphitheatre* (Museum of London Archaeology, 2011).

Gunnersbury Park Museum: HEMN 397917; HEMN 397919; HEMN.
www.visitgunnersbury.org/museum

Hackney Museum: www.hackney-museum.hackney.gov.uk

Headstone Manor and Museum: TLMAS 59 (2008) 61–81.
www.headstonemanor.org

Highgate Roman Kiln: HEMN 401396.
www.highgateromankiln.org.uk

Huggin Hill: HEL 1001981; LA 6 (1989) 59–62; TLMAS 27 (1976) 3–29.

Innholders' Hall: HEL 1002028.

Institute of Archaeology Collections (UCL): www.ucl.ac.uk/culture/institute-archaeology

Ironmonger Lane: HEL 1193231; HEMN 405118; HEMN 1146511.

Islington Museum: www.friendsofim.com

Keston Roman Villa & Tombs: AC 69 (1955) 96–116; HEL 1002024; JRS 12 (1922) 240–287.
Philip, B., *The Roman Villa site at Keston, Kent (First report 1968–78)* (Kent Archaeological Rescue Unit, 1991).
Philip, B., *The Roman Villa Site at Keston, Kent Second Report Excavations 1967 & 1979–99* (Kent Archaeological Rescue Unit, 1999).

Leadenhall Market: BRIT 21 (1990) 53–97; HEL 1002035; JRS 11 (1921) 200–244; JRS 15 (1925) 223–252; JRS 42 (1952) 86–109; LA 5 (1986) 151; LA 6 (1990) 179–187.

The Liberty of Southwark: www.thelibertyofsouthwark.com

London Mithraeum: HEL 1391846; HEMN 404539.
Bryan, J. et al., *Archaeology Bloomberg* (Museum of London Archaeology, 2017).
Tomlin, R. S. O., *Roman London's first voices Writing tablets from the Bloomberg excavations, 2010–14* (Museum of London Archaeology, 2016).
www.londonmithraeum.com

London Stone: HEL 1286846; HEMN 405249.

London Wall: www.colatcoat.org.uk/_assets/doc/london-wall-walk-guide.pdf
www.londonmymind.com/london-wall-walk

London Wall Car Park: HEL 1018885.

Ludgate Hill: HEL 1002052; HEMN 1166001; HEMN 405063; HEMN 966523; HEMN 966521; HEMN 966523; LA 14 (2014) 3–10.

Moorgate: HEL 1002051; HEMN 966484; HEMN 405120.

Morden Park Mound: HEL 1002011 HEMN 400671.

Mount Clare: HEL 1184436.
www.heritageoflondon.org/projects/mount-clare-temple

Museum of Croydon: www.museumofcroydon.com

Museum of London: www.museumoflondon.org.uk/museum-london

Museum of London Docklands: www.museumoflondon.org.uk/museum-london-docklands

Natural History Museum: www.nhm.ac.uk/our-science/collections/palaeontology-collections/london-human-remains-collection/iron-age-roman-sites-collection.html
www.nhm.ac.uk/our-science/collections/palaeontology-collections/london-human-remains-collection/london-wall-collection.html

Noble Street Garden: HEL 1018890.

Old Bailey (Central Criminal Courts): HEL 1018884; HEMN 405348; HEMN 962978; HEMN 1460760.

Old Kent Road Mural: HEL 1442278.

Osterley Park Roman Bridge: HEL 1079401; HEMN 119533.

Petrie Museum of Egyptian Archaeology (UCL): www.ucl.ac.uk/culture/petrie-museum

Plantation Place Roman Fort: BRIT 49 (2018) 466–467.
Dunwoodie, L., Haward, C., Pitt, K., *An Early Roman Fort and Urban Development on Londinium's Eastern Hill: Excavations at Plantation Place, City of London, 1997–2003* (Museum of London Archaeology, 2015).

Postman's Park (King Edward Street): HEL 1018883.
www.sketchfab.com/3d-models/london-roman-wall-postmans-park-a0cf92766ea74e0187749c3dd93bc0d8

Pudding Lane: HEMN 405200; HEMN 405198.

Queenhithe Dock | Smith's Wharf: HEL 1001994.

Romford Golf Course: HEL 1001987; HEMN 965559.

Royal Arsenal (Woolwich): HEMN 213679; HEMN 111404.

St Alphage Churchyard: HEL 1018886.

St Botolph-without-Bishopgate Church: HEL 1064732; HEMN 966427.

St Bride's Church: HEL 1064657; HEMN 404894.
www.stbrides.com

St Magnus the Martyr Church: HEL 1064601; HEMN 141421.
www.stmagnusmartyr.org.uk

St Mary Axe (The Gherkin): BRIT 27 (1996) 430; BRIT 28 (1997) 440.

Shadwell: HEL 1456951; HEMN 966559; HEMN 98837; HEMN 136373; HEMN 77643; HEMN 78247; LA 12 (2010) 298; LA 13 (2013) 271–275.
Douglas, A., Gerrard, J., Sudds, B., *A Roman Settlement and Bath House At Shadwell. Excavations at Tobacco Dock and Babe Ruth Restaurant, the Highway, London* (Pre-Construct Archaeology, 2011).

Sir John Soane Museum: www.soane.org

Skinners' Hall: HEL 1002031.

Southwark Cathedral: HEL 144278; HEMN 96384; HEMN 1506784; HEMN 213909; HEMN 148283; HEMN 102362; HEMN 111694; HEMN 105674; HEMN 129617; HEMN 108035; HEMN 126806; HEMN 142005.
www.cathedral.southwark.anglican.org/visiting/exhibitions-and-installations/romano-southwarkSouthwarksouthward-online-exhibition

Southwark Heritage Centre and Walworth Library: www.heritage.southwark.gov.uk
www.heritage.southwark.gov.uk/collections/7727/roman-archaeology-londinium/objects

Spitalfields: McKenzie, M., Thomas, C., *In the northern cemetery of Roman London: excavations at Spitalfields Market, London E1, 1991–2007* (Museum of London Archaeology, 2020).

Strand Lane Roman Baths: HEL 1237102; LA 2 (1975) 249.
www.heritagerecords.nationaltrust.org.uk/HBSMR/MonRecord.aspx?uid=MNA129529
Trapp, M., *New Light on the Strand Lane 'Bath' in National Trust Historic Houses and Collections Annual* (National Trust, 2012)

Sudbury Stone: HEL 1189574; HEMN 398122.

The Three Tuns (Aldgate): www.bestcitypubs.co.uk/three-tuns-aldgate

Tower of London | Tower Hill West: HEL 1001980; HEL 1002061; HEMN 405272; HEMN 145741; HEMN 77015; JRS 1 (1911) 141–172; JRS 46 (1956) 139–140; LA 3 (1978) 171–176.

Trinity Place: HEL 1002062. See also Cooper's Row.

Trinity Square | The Emperor Trajan Statue: HEL 1002063; HEL 1357518; HEMN 405278; HEMN 134872; HEMN 140793; HEMN 133789.

Twickenham Museum: www.twickenham-museum.org.uk

Valence House Museum: www.valencehousecollections.co.uk

Vestry House Museum: www.vestryhousemuseum.org.uk

Victoria & Albert Museum: www.vam.ac.uk

Westminster Abbey: HEMN 965804; HEMN 117610; HEMN 127510; HEMN 123154; HEMN 147768; HEMN 119228; HEMN 95529; HEMN 140592. www.westminster-abbey.org

Winchester Palace | Clink Street | Winchester Square: HEL 1002054; HEMN 117582; HEMN 143448; HEMN 131845; HEMN 132862.
Yule, B., *A Prestigious Roman building complex on the Southwark waterfront: excavations at Winchester Palace, London, 1983–90* (Museum of London Archaeology Service, 2005).
www.english-heritage.org.uk/visit/places/winchester-palace

Beyond London

Bath: Davenport, P., *Roman BathRoman Baths: A New History and Archaeology of Aquae Sulis* (The History Press, 2021).

Canterbury: Harmsworth, A., *Roman Canterbury: A Journey into the Past* (Canterbury Archaeological Trust, 1994).

Colchester: Chittenden, J., *Roman Colchester: Exploring Britain's First City* (jc3dvis, 2022).
Crummy, P., *City of Victory: The Story of Colchester – Britain's First Roman Town* (Colchester Archaeological Trust, 1997).

Exeter: Rippon, S., Holbrook, N., *Roman and Medieval Exeter and their Hinterlands: From Isca to Excester: A Place in Time* (Oxbow Books, 2021)

Fishbourne Roman Palace and Gardens: Cunliffe, B., *Fishbourne Roman Palace* (Tempus History and Archaeology, 1998).
Rudkin, D., *Fishbourne Roman Palace: An Illustrated Family Guide* (Sussex Archaeological Society, 2000).

Hadrian's Wall: Tibbs, A., *A Short Guide to Hadrian's Wall* (Amberley Publishing, 2022).

Lincoln: Jones, M., *Roman Lincoln: Conquest, Colony and Capital* (Tempus, 2002).

St Albans: Niblett, R., *Verulamium: The Roman City of St Albans* (The History Press, 2001).
St Albans Museums, *Verulamium Guide Book* (St Albans Museums).

Saxon Shore Forts: English Heritage, *Guidebook: Richborough and Reculver* (English Heritage, 2012).
Fields, N., *Rome's Saxon Shore: Coastal Defences of Roman Britain AD 250–500* (Osprey Publishing, 2006).

Scotland: Tibbs, A., *Beyond the Empire: A Guide to Scotland's Roman Remains* (Robert Hale, 2019).

Silchester: English Heritage, *Guidebook: Silchester Roman Town* (English Heritage, 2016).
Fulford, M., *A Guide to Silchester: The Roman Town of Calleva Atrebatum* (Calleva Trust, 2002).

Welwyn Roman Baths: Rook, T., *The Story of Welwyn Roman Baths* (Hertfordshire Histories, 2002).

York: Parker, A., *The Archaeology of Roman York* (Amberley Publishing, 2019).

Index of Places